Masahiro Yagisawa

Fully Homomorphic Encryption without bootstrapping

Masahiro Yagisawa

Fully Homomorphic Encryption without bootstrapping

Fully homomorphic encyption with multivariate polynomials on octonion ring

LAP LAMBERT Academic Publishing

Impressum / Imprint
Bibliografische Information der Deutschen Nationalbibliothek: Die Deutsche Nationalbibliothek verzeichnet diese Publikation in der Deutschen Nationalbibliografie; detaillierte bibliografische Daten sind im Internet über http://dnb.d-nb.de abrufbar.
Alle in diesem Buch genannten Marken und Produktnamen unterliegen warenzeichen-, marken- oder patentrechtlichem Schutz bzw. sind Warenzeichen oder eingetragene Warenzeichen der jeweiligen Inhaber. Die Wiedergabe von Marken, Produktnamen, Gebrauchsnamen, Handelsnamen, Warenbezeichnungen u.s.w. in diesem Werk berechtigt auch ohne besondere Kennzeichnung nicht zu der Annahme, dass solche Namen im Sinne der Warenzeichen- und Markenschutzgesetzgebung als frei zu betrachten wären und daher von jedermann benutzt werden dürften.

Bibliographic information published by the Deutsche Nationalbibliothek: The Deutsche Nationalbibliothek lists this publication in the Deutsche Nationalbibliografie; detailed bibliographic data are available in the Internet at http://dnb.d-nb.de.
Any brand names and product names mentioned in this book are subject to trademark, brand or patent protection and are trademarks or registered trademarks of their respective holders. The use of brand names, product names, common names, trade names, product descriptions etc. even without a particular marking in this work is in no way to be construed to mean that such names may be regarded as unrestricted in respect of trademark and brand protection legislation and could thus be used by anyone.

Coverbild / Cover image: www.ingimage.com

Verlag / Publisher:
LAP LAMBERT Academic Publishing
ist ein Imprint der / is a trademark of
OmniScriptum GmbH & Co. KG
Heinrich-Böcking-Str. 6-8, 66121 Saarbrücken, Deutschland / Germany
Email: info@lap-publishing.com

Herstellung: siehe letzte Seite /
Printed at: see last page
ISBN: 978-3-659-47233-6

PREFACE

We use the cryptosystem for the information security. It is said that
·key agreement protocols (KAP),
· encryption
· digital signature
are the fundamental cryptographic primitives.

KAP allow some parties to exchange information each other through the insecure communication line. They obtain a common session key, which they use for later secure communication. The plaintext is enciphered into a ciphertext by using the common session key and the ciphertext is deciphered into the plain text by using the same common session key.Thus, KAP are thought to be the basic primitive for constructing the secure communication.

Since Diffie and Hellman [0.1] proposed the concept of KAP and the public key cryptosystems (PKC) in 1976, various KAP and PKC were proposed.
Typical examples of KAP are almost based on the discrete logarithm problem over finite fields (DLP) or on the elliptic curve discrete logarithm problem (ECDLP).

Typical examples of KAP are classified as follows.
1) Diffie-Hellman KAP based on the discrete logarithm problem on the finite multiplicative group,
2) Authenticated KAP based on the discrete logarithm problem on the elliptic curve,
3) Identity-based KAP based on the bilinear map such as Weil paring and Tate paring, and so on.

Typical examples of PKC are classified as follows.
1) RSA cryptosystem [0.2] based on factoring problem ,
2) ElGamal cryptosystem [0.3] based on the discrete logarithm problem on the finite multiplicative group,
3) the elliptic curve cryptosystem based on the discrete logarithm problem on the elliptic curve[0.4],
4) multivariate public key cryptosystems (MPKC)[0.5] ,
and so on.

It is said that

· the problem of factoring large integers,
· the problem of solving discrete logarithms over multiplicative group
· the problem of computing elliptic curve discrete logarithms
are efficiently solved in a polynomial time by the quantum computers.

It is thought that MPKC is immune from the attack of the quantum computers. But MPKC proposed until now almost adopt the multivariate quadratic equations because of avoiding the explosion of key length.

PKC need the trap-door one way function in deciphering that may be the weak point for the cryptosystems. But KAP do not always need the trap-door one way function. Then it is said that KAP are more robust than PKC in this sense.

I have already proposed some schemes of KAP based on the difficulty of solving the multivariate equations of high degree over finite field [0.6][0.7][0.8]. As the enciphering function these schemes adopt the polynomials over the quaternion ring in which the multiplicative operation is non-commutative.

Encryption is classified into symmetric key encryption and public key encryption.

Symmetric-key algorithms are a class of algorithms for cryptography that use the same cryptographic keys for both encryption of plaintext and decryption of ciphertext. The keys may be identical or there may be a simple transformation to go between the two keys. The keys, in practice, represent a shared secret between two or more parties that can be used to maintain a private information link. This requirement that both parties have access to the secret key is one of the main drawbacks of symmetric key encryption, in comparison to public-key encryption.

Public-key cryptography, also known as asymmetric cryptography, is a class of cryptographic algorithms which requires two separate keys, one of which is secret (or private) and one of which is public. Although different, the two parts of this key pair are mathematically linked. The public key is used to encrypt plaintext or to verify a digital signature; whereas the private key is used to decrypt ciphertext or to create a digital signature. The term "asymmetric" stems from the use of different keys to perform these opposite functions, each the inverse of the other – as contrasted with conventional ("symmetric") cryptography which relies on the same key to perform both.

Public-key algorithms are based on mathematical problems which currently admit no efficient solution that are inherent in certain integer factorization, discrete logarithm, and elliptic curve relationships. It is computationally easy for a user to generate their own public and private key-pair and to use them for encryption and decryption. The strength lies in the fact that it is "impossible" (computationally infeasible) for a properly generated private key to be determined from its corresponding public key. Thus the public key may be published without compromising security, whereas the private key must not be revealed to anyone not authorized to read messages or perform digital signatures. Public key algorithms, unlike symmetric key algorithms, do not require a secure initial exchange of one (or more) secret keys between the parties.

A digital signature is a mathematical scheme for demonstrating the authenticity of a digital message or document. A valid digital signature gives a recipient reason to believe that the message was created by a known sender, such that the sender cannot deny having sent the message (authentication and non-repudiation) and that the message was not altered in transit (integrity). Digital signatures are commonly used for software distribution, financial transactions, and in other cases where it is important to detect forgery or tampering. In future I will describe the digital signature scheme as the signcryption scheme based on the octonion ring or fully homomorphic signature scheme based on the octonion ring.

Here I describe on **fully homomorphic encryption** (FHE).

Fully homomorphic encryption (FHE) is the cryptosystem which supports both addition and multiplication (thereby preserving the ring structure of the plaintexts). Using such a scheme, we can construct the programs which may be run on encryptions of their inputs to produce an encryption of their output. Since such a program never decrypts its input, it can be run by an untrusted party without revealing its inputs and internal state. The existence of the cryptosystems which have efficiency and fully homomorphism would bring great practical implications in the outsourcing of private computations, for instance, in the context of cloud computing.

Fully homomorphic encryption is a form of encryption which allows specific types of computations to be carried out on ciphertext and generate an encrypted result which, when decrypted, matches the result of operations performed on the plaintext.

This is a desirable feature in modern communication system architectures. Fully homomorphic encryption would allow the chaining together of different services without exposing the data to each of those services. For example a chain of different services from different companies could calculate
1) the tax,
2) the currency exchange rate,
3) shipping on a transaction

without exposing the unencrypted data to each of those services.

Fully homomorphic encryption schemes are malleable by design. The fully homomorphic property of various cryptosystems can be used to create secure voting systems, collision-resistant hash functions, private information retrieval schemes and enable widespread use of cloud computing by ensuring the confidentiality of processed data.

There are several efficient, partially homomorphic cryptosystems, and a number of fully homomorphic, but less efficient cryptosystems. Although a cryptosystem which is unintentionally homomorphic can be subject to attacks on this basis, if treated carefully homomorphism can also be used to perform computations securely.

With fully homomorphic encryption, a company could encrypt its entire database of e-mails and upload it to a cloud. Then it could use the cloud-stored data as desired—for example, to calculate the stochastic value of stored data. The results would be downloaded and decrypted without ever exposing the details of a single e-mail.

In 2009 Craig Gentry is creating an encryption system [0.9] that could solve the problem keeping many organizations from using cloud computing to analyze and mine data: it's too much of a security risk to give a public cloud provider such as Amazon or Google access to unencrypted data.

The problem is that while data can be sent to and from a cloud provider's data center in encrypted form, the servers that power a cloud can't do any work on it that way. Gentry has shown that it is possible to analyze data without decrypting it. The key is to encrypt the data in such a way that performing a mathematical operation on the encrypted information and then decrypting the result produces the same answer as performing an analogous operation on the unencrypted data. The correspondence between the operations on unencrypted data and the operations to be performed on encrypted data is known as a **homomorphism**. "In principle," says Gentry, "something like this could be used to secure operations over the Internet."

Gentry began tackling fully homomorphic encryption in 2008. At first he was able to perform only a few basic operations on encrypted data before his system started producing garbage. Unfortunately, a task like finding a piece of text in an e-mail requires chaining together thousands of basic operations. His solution was to use a second layer of encryption, essentially to protect intermediate results when the system broke down and needed to be reset.

It is said that "the problem of how to create true fully homomorphic encryption has been debated for more than 30 years, and Gentry was the first person who got it right and figured out how to make the math work" and "however, because Gentry's scheme with **bootstrapping** technique currently requires a huge amount of computation, there's a long way to go before it will be widely usable".

Gentry acknowledges that the way he applied the double layer of encryption was "a bit of a hack" and that the system runs too slowly for practical use, but he is working on optimizing it for specific applications such as searching databases for records. He estimates that these applications could be ready for the market in five to 10 years.

It is said that "All known FHE schemes are based on the hardness of lattice problems. Can we construct FHE from other, perhaps number-theoretic assumptions? How about the hardness of factoring or discrete logarithms?".

The fully homomorhic encryption scheme that runs fast for practical use is not proposed until now.

I propose the **fully homomorphic encryption scheme** without bootstrappig which does not base on the hardness of lattice problem , but bases on the hardness of solving the multivariate algebraic equations on octonion [0.10] ring and run fast for practical use.

In this book, I describe the **new fully homomorhic encryption scheme** that I have found in last year by using multivariate polynomials over octonion ring O without the explosion of the key length. The security of these systems is based on the computational difficulty to solve the multivariate algebraic equations over the finite field Fq. I have also found the fully homomorphic *public key* encryption scheme and fully homomorphic *signature* scheme, but I will describe these schemes in the near future.

To break these cryptosystems it is thought that we probably need to solve the multivariate algebraic equations that are equal to solving the NP complete problem. Then it is thought that these systems are immune from the attacks by the quantum computers.

In chapter 1, the preliminaries for reading later chapters are explained. First, the explanation on a group, ring and field is presented. Second, the mathematical preparation on the octonion ring is explained as the octonion ring is the basic ring of the cryptosystems described in the later chapter. Third, polynomial ring in several variables is mentioned simply. Next re-encryption scheme is mentioned which is used in chapter 4. The property of the fully homomorphic enciphering and deciphering functions is mentioned. And quantum computer is mentioned which is said to be able to break the RSA cryptosystem based on the problem of factorization synthesis number , the elliptic cryptosystem based on the elliptic curve discrete logarithm problem and so on. At the end of this chapter a simple explanation on Gröbner basis attack is described.

In chapter 2 previous works about fully homomorphic encryption are mentioned.

In chapter 3 two simple examples of fully homomorphic encryption on octonion ring are mentioned.

In chapter 4 fully homomorphic encryption scheme using the multivariate polynomials over the finite field Fq is constructed concretely. This system has the computational difficulty to solve the multivariate algebraic equations over the finite field Fq that is equal to solving the NP complete problem. At the beginning the summary is placed. Preliminaries for octonion operation are described for the understanding of the readers. In the next we describe the concept of proposed fully homomorphic encryption scheme, proposed fully homomorphic data-processing procedure and the re-encryption scheme.

At end o f chapter 4 the conceptual charts of the proposed fully homomorphic data-processing procedure and re-encryption scheme are attached.

A bibliography is provided after chapter 4.

Finally appendix A, B, C and D are attached.

Chapters are divided into Sections, which are numbered chapter-wise. Chapter 4 has the summary at the beginning of the chapter and the conclusion remarks at the end of the chapter. The equation number (c.e) refers to the e-th equation in chapter c.

I typed the manuscript with utmost care, but some oversight or discrepancy is thought to exist yet. I shall acknowledge thankfully the oversight or discrepancy brought to the notice by inquisitive readers.

I wish to accord here my warm gratitude to the publisher (Lambert Academic, Germany) for kindly providing an opportunity to accomplish the task.

Finally I would like to thank my wife, *Momoe,* for supporting me mentally through the writing this book. I would like to dedicate this book to her.

Yokohama (Japan): (March 11, 2015)   Masahiro Yagisawa

CONTENTS

Section	Sub-Section	Title	Page
		PREFACE...1-6	
		CHAPTER 1: PRELIMINARIES...................9-21	
1.		Group, ring and field...9	
2.		Octonion ring over Fq..10	
3.		Polynomial ring in several variables 14	
4.		Re-encryption scheme...18	
5.		Fully homomorphic enciphering/deciphering function....................20	
6.		Quantum computer.. 20	
7.		Gröbner basis attack.. 21	

CHAPTER 2: PREVIOUS FULLY HOMOMORPHIC ENCRYPTION SCHEMES...22-24

CHAPTER 3: EXAMPLES OF FULLY HOMOMORPHIC ENCIPHERING FUNCTION ON OCTONION RING............................25-27

| 1. | | Example 1...25 | |
| 2. | | Example 2...26 | |

CHAPTER 4: PROPOSED FULLY HOMOMORPHIC ENCRYPTION..28-66

		Summary...28	
1.		Introduction...28	
2.		Preliminaries for octonion operation.................................29	
	2.1	Multiplication and addition on the octonion ring O....................29	
	2.2	Order of the element in O...................................... 30	
	2.3.	Property of multiplication over octonion ring O.........................31	
3.		Concept of proposed fully homomorphic encryption scheme.........41	
	3.1	Definition of homomorphic encryption.................................41	
	3.2	Definition of fully homomorphic encryption.............................42	
	3.3	Proposed fully homomorphic enciphering/deciphering functions.... 42	
	3.4	Elements on octonion ring assumption EOR($k;q$).....................43	
	3.5	Syntax of proposed algorithms 43	

3.6　　Addition/subtraction scheme on ciphertexts...........................44

3.7　　Multiplication scheme on ciphertexts...............................45

3.8　　Inverse of $E(M,X)$...45

3.9　　Division scheme on ciphertexts.................................48

3.10　Property of proposed fully homomorphic encryption................48

4.　　　Proposed fully homomorphic data-processing procedure............49

5.　　　Proposed re-encryption scheme.....................................53

6.　　　Analysis of proposed scheme..54

6.1　　Computing plaintext M and A_i (i=1,...,k)　from coefficients of

ciphertext $E(M,X;A)$ to be published................................54

6.2　　Computing plaintext M_i and d_{ijk} (i,j,k=0,...,7)...........................56

7.　　　The size of the modulus q and the complexity for enciphering/

deciphering...58

8.　　　Conclusion of chapter 4...59

9.　　　Concidering composition of plaintext..............................59

Fig.4.1 the conceptual chart of the proposed fully homomorphic encryption

scheme...65

Fig.4.2 the conceptual chart of the proposed re-encryption scheme..........66

BIBLIOGRAPHY..67-68

Appendix A...69

Appendix B...70

Appendix C...71

Appendix D...74

CHAPTER 1

PRELIMINARIES

§1. Group, ring and field

We explain a *group,* a *ring*, and a *field* simply.

A *group* is a set of elements, together with an operation performed on pairs of these elements such that,

1) When two elements of the set as arguments are given, the operation always returns an element of the set as its result. It is thus fully defined, and closed over the set.

2) One element of the set is an identity element. Thus, let $\otimes$ be the operation. There is some element of the set e such that for any other element of the set x,

$$e \otimes x = x \otimes e = x.$$

3) Every element of the set has an inverse element. Let p be any element of the set. Then there is another element q such that

$$p \otimes q = q \otimes p = e.$$

4) The operation $\otimes$ is associative. That is, for any three elements of the set,

$$(a \otimes b) \otimes c = a \otimes (b \otimes c).$$

There are many different kinds of finite *groups*, in which there are some *groups* with very complex structure. Most *groups* belong to families of *groups* with an infinite number of members. Thus, addition modulo 5 yields the cyclic *group* of order 5, and there are cyclic *groups* of every integer order starting with 2.

A *ring* is a set of elements with two operations. Let $+$ be the one operation to be like addition, and let $*$ be the other to be like multiplication. The operations have the following properties:

1) The elements of the *ring*, together with the addition operation, form a *group*.
2) Addition is commutative. That is, for any two elements of the set p and q,
$$p + q = q + p.$$
3) The multiplication operation is associative.

4) Multiplication distributes over addition: that is, for any three elements of the *group* a, b and c,

$$a * (b + c) = (a * b) + (a * c).$$

For example, addition and multiplication modulo 5 yield *rings*. Matrix multiplication also leads to *rings* as well.

A *field* is a *ring* in which the elements, other than the identity element for addition, and the multiplication operator, also form a *group*.

There are only two kinds of finite *fields* denoted by Fq. One kind is the *field* formed by addition and multiplication modulo a prime number. The other kind of finite *field* has a number of elements that is a power of a prime number. The addition operator consists of multiple independent additions modulo that prime. The elements of the *field* can be thought of as polynomials whose coefficients are numbers modulo that prime. In that case, multiplication is polynomial multiplication, where not only the coefficients are modulo that prime, but the polynomials are modulo a special kind of polynomial, known as a primitive polynomial. All finite *fields*, but particularly those of this second kind, are known as *Galois fields*.

§2. Octonion ring over Fq

Let q be a prime larger than 2.
Let O be the octonion ring over Fq. Every element of O can be written as a linear combination of these basis elements $1, e_1, \ldots, e_7$.
That is,

$$c_0 1 + c_1 e_1 + c_2 e_2 + c_3 e_3 + c_4 e_4 + c_5 e_5 + c_6 e_6 + c_7 e_7 \text{ where } c_0, \ldots, c_7 \in Fq.$$

The basis element 1 will be the identity element of O, meaning that multiplication by 1 does nothing, and for this reason, elements of O are usually written

$$c_0 + c_1 e_1 + c_2 e_2 + c_3 e_3 + c_4 e_4 + c_5 e_5 + c_6 e_6 + c_7 e_7,$$

supressing the basis element 1. When this basis is given, non-associative octonion multiplication is defined by first defining the products of basis elements and then defining all other products using the distributive law.

If we select 2 as q, the multiplication between the two or three elements of O has not the non-commutative and non-associative property. Then, in this book we don't adopt 2 as q.

We mention multiplication of basis elements as follows.

When multiplying octonions, there are rules for combining the different imaginary operators. The multiplication rules can be shown by the 'fano plane' (see **Fig.1.1**).

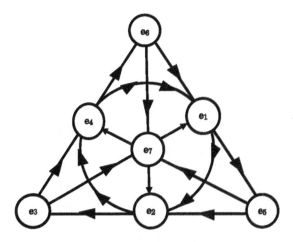

Fig.1.1 fano plane

It works as follows, if you want to multiply e_3 by e_7 for example, look at the diagram and find the line that joins them and you will see that there is a third point on the line, in this case e_1. Following the arrows, you go from e_3 to e_7 to e_1 so e_3 $e_7 = e_1$ reversing the order of the multiplicands gives minus the result so if the order on the line is reversed then put a negative sign in front of the result.

The square of any imaginary operator is **-1** such that

$$e_1{}^2 = e_2{}^2 = e_3{}^2 = e_4{}^2 = e_5{}^2 = e_6{}^2 = e_7{}^2 = \text{-}1$$

where e_i ($i=1,\ldots,7$) are basis elements of O, and all the possible products of e_l and e_j($i,j=1,\ldots,7$) are determined.

Table 1.1 Multiplication table for octonions

	1	e_1	e_2	e_3	e_4	e_5	e_6	e_7
1	1	e_1	e_2	e_3	e_4	e_5	e_6	e_7
e_1	e_1	**-1**	e_4	e_7	$-e_2$	e_6	$-e_5$	$-e_3$
e_2	e_2	$-e_4$	**-1**	e_5	e_1	$-e_3$	e_7	$-e_6$
e_3	e_3	$-e_7$	$-e_5$	**-1**	e_6	e_2	$-e_4$	e_1
e_4	e_4	e_2	$-e_1$	$-e_6$	**-1**	e_7	e_3	$-e_5$
e_5	e_5	$-e_6$	e_3	$-e_2$	$-e_7$	**-1**	e_1	e_4
e_6	e_6	e_5	$-e_7$	e_4	$-e_3$	$-e_1$	**-1**	e_2
e_7	e_7	e_3	e_6	$-e_1$	e_5	$-e_4$	$-e_2$	**-1**

The above definition is not unique, but is only one of 480 possible definitions for octonion multiplication with $e_0 = \mathbf{1}$. The others can be obtained by permuting and changing the signs of the non-scalar basis elements. The 480 different algebras are isomorphic, and there is rarely a need to consider which particular multiplication rule is used. Each of these 480 definitions is invariant up to signs under some 7-cycle of the points (1234567), and for each 7-cycle there are four definitions, differing by signs and reversal of order. A common choice is to use the definition invariant under the 7-cycle (1234567) with $e_1 e_2 = e_4$ as it is particularly easy to remember the multiplication.

Here I show some examples of the multiplication. From table1.1 we obtain

$$(((((e_1 e_2)e_3)e_4)e_5)e_6 = (((e_4 e_3)e_4)e_5)e_6 = ((-e_6 e_4)e_5)e_6 = (-(-e_3 e_5))e_6 = -(-e_2 e_6) = -(-e_7) = e_7.$$

The other products can be determined by similar methods, resulting in

$$(((((e_2 e_3)e_4)e_5)e_6)e_7 = (((e_5 e_4)e_5)e_6)e_7 = ((-e_7 e_5)e_6)e_7 = (-(-e_4 e_6))e_7 = -(-e_3 e_7) = -(-e_1) = e_1,$$

$$(((((e_3 e_4)e_5)e_6)e_7)e_1 = (((e_6 e_5)e_6)e_7)e_1 = ((-e_1 e_6)e_7)e_1 = (-(-e_5 e_7))e_1 = -(-e_4 e_1) = -(-e_2) = e_2,$$

$$\dots \qquad \dots \qquad \dots \qquad \dots$$

$((((e_7e_1)e_2)e_3)e_4)e_5=(((e_3e_2)e_3)e_4)e_5 =((-e_5e_3)e_4)e_5 =(-(-e_2e_4))e_5 =-(-e_1e_5)=-(-e_6)=e_6.$

For two elements

$$a=a_0 + a_1e_1+ a_2e_2+ a_3e_3 + a_4e_4+ a_5e_5+ a_6e_6+ a_7e_7$$

and

$$b=b_0 + b_1 e_1+ b_2e_2+ b_3e_3 + b_4e_4+ b_5e_5+ b_6e_6+ b_7e_7,$$

addition $a+b$ mod q is determined as follows.

$$a+b \text{ mod } q$$

$= a_0 + a_1e_1+ a_2e_2+ a_3e_3 + a_4e_4+ a_5e_5+ a_6e_6+ a_7e_7 + b_0 + b_1 e_1+ b_2e_2+ b_3e_3 + b_4e_4+ b_5e_5+ b_6e_6+ b_7e_7$

$= (a_0 + b_0 \text{ mod } q)+ (a_1+b_1 \text{ mod } q)e_1+ (a_2+b_2 \text{ mod } q)e_2+ (a_3+b_3 \text{ mod } q)e_3$

$+(a_4+b_4 \text{ mod } q)e_4+ (a_5+b_5 \text{ mod } q)e_5+ (a_6+b_6 \text{ mod } q)e_6+(a_7+b_7 \text{ mod } q)e_7.$

Their product ab is determined by the products of the basis elements and the distributive low. The distributive law makes it possible to expand the product so that it is a sum of products of basis elements. This gives the following expression:

ab mod q

$=(a_0 + a_1e_1+ a_2e_2+ a_3e_3 + a_4e_4+ a_5e_5+ a_6e_6+ a_7e_7)(b_0 + b_1 e_1+ b_2e_2+ b_3e_3 + b_4e_4+ b_5e_5+ b_6e_6+ b_7e_7).$

Now the basis elements can be multiplied using the rules given above to get

$=(a_0b_0-a_1b_1- a_2b_2- a_3b_3-a_4b_4- a_5b_5-a_6b_6-a_7b_7 \text{ mod } q)$

$+(a_0b_1+a_1b_0+a_2b_4+a_3b_7-a_4b_2+a_5b_6-a_6b_5-a_7b_3 \text{ mod } q) \, e_1$

$+(a_0b_2-a_1b_4+a_2b_0+a_3b_5+a_4b_1-a_5b_3+a_6b_7-a_7b_6 \text{ mod } q) \, e_2,$

$+(a_0b_3-a_1b_7-a_2b_5+a_3b_0+a_4b_6+a_5b_2-a_6b_4+a_7b_1 \text{ mod } q) \, e_3$

$+(a_0b_4+a_1b_2-a_2b_1-a_3b_6+a_4b_0+a_5b_7+a_6b_3-a_7b_5 \text{ mod } q) \, e_4$

$+(a_0b_5-a_1b_6+a_2b_3-a_3b_2-a_4b_7+a_5b_0+a_6b_1+a_7b_4 \text{ mod } q) \, e_5$

$$+(a_0b_6+a_1b_5-a_2b_7+a_3b_4-a_4b_3-a_5b_1+a_6b_0+a_7b_2 \bmod q)\, e_6$$
$$+(a_0b_7+a_1b_3+a_2b_6-a_3b_1+a_4b_5-a_5b_4-a_6b_2+a_7b_0 \bmod q)\, e_7.$$

We define ordered list form which we call the element expression as follows. Using the basis $\mathbf{1}$, e_i ($i=1,\ldots,7$) of O makes it possible to write O as a set of octuple (8-tuple):

$$O=\{(a_0,a_1,a_2,a_3,a_4,a_5,a_6,a_7)/a_i\in Fq(i=0,\ldots,7)\,\}.$$

Then the basis elements $\mathbf{1}$, e_i ($i=1,\ldots,7$) correspond to $(1,0,0,0,0,0,0,0)$, $(0,1,0,0,0,0,0,0)$, $(0,0,1,0,0,0,0,0)$, $(0,0,0,1,0,0,0,0)$, $(0,0,0,0,1,0,0,0)$, $(0,0,0,0,0,1,0,0)$, $(0,0,0,0,0,0,1,0)$ and $(0,0,0,0,0,0,0,1)$.

In general multiplication of $\mathbf{a}=(a_0,a_1,a_2,a_3,\ldots,a_7)$ and $\mathbf{b}=(b_0,b_1,b_2,b_3,\ldots,b_7)$ is non-commutative.
$\mathbf{b}$ is commutative to given $\mathbf{a}$ under the condition that

$$a_ib_j-a_jb_i \bmod q = 0 \;(i<j;\ i,j=1,\ldots,7).$$

That is, $\mathbf{b}$ to be commutative to $\mathbf{a}$ is given as follows.

$$\mathbf{b}=(b_0,\ ra_1,\ ra_2,\ ra_3,\ldots,ra_7),$$

where

$$r\in Fq.$$

We describe the property of octonion such as non-associativity A, B and $C\in O$

$$(AB)C\neq A(BC) \bmod q \;\in O$$

and so on at " **Chapter 4　§2.3. Property of multiplication over octonion ring O**".

§3. Polynomial ring over octonion ring in several variables

A polynomial P in n variables $X_1,\ldots,X_n$ with coefficients in a ring O is defined as follows. For any multi-index $a=(a_0,\ldots,a_{n-1})$, where each a_i is a non-negative integer, let

$$X^a:=\prod_{i=0}^{n-1}X_i^{a_i}=X_0^{a_0}X_1^{a_1}\ldots X_{n-1}^{a_{n-1}},$$

$$P_a := P_{a_0 a_1 \dots a_{n-1}} \in O$$

The product X^{α} is called the monomial of multi-degree a. A polynomial P is a finite linear combination of monomials with coefficients in O such that

$$P := \sum_a P_a X^a$$

and finitely many coefficients P_a are different from 0. The degree of a monomial X^a, frequently denoted $|a|$, is defined as

$$|a| := \sum_{i=0}^{n-1} a_i,$$

and the degree of a polynomial P is the largest degree of a monomial occurring with non-zero coefficient in the expansion of P. Polynomials P in n variables with coefficients in O form a non-commutative ring denoted $O[X_0, \dots, X_{n-1}]$, or sometimes $O[X]$, where X is a symbol representing the full set of variables, $X = (X_0, \dots, X_{n-1})$, and called the polynomial ring in n variables.

As an example, we notice the following polynomials.

$$F(X) := A_1(A_2(\dots(A_k X)\dots)) \bmod q \in O[X],$$

where

$A_i \in O$ is the coefficients ($i=1, \dots, k$) and $X = (x_0, \dots, x_7) \in O$ is a variable,

$F(X)$ has the element expression as follows.

$$F(X) = A_1(A_2(\dots(A_k X)\dots)),$$

$$= (\, a_{00}x_0 + a_{01}x_1 + \dots + a_{07}x_7,$$

$$a_{10}x_0 + a_{11}x_1 + \dots + a_{17}x_7$$

$$\dots \qquad \dots \qquad \dots$$

$$a_{70}x_0 + a_{71}x_1 + \dots + a_{77}x_7\,) \bmod q$$

with $a_{ij} \in Fq$ ($i,j = 0, \dots, 7$).

When $X=M=(m_0,\ldots,m_7)\in \boldsymbol{O}$, $F(M)$ is given such that

$$F(M)=A_1(A_2(\ldots(A_kM)\ldots)),$$

$$=(\ a_{00}m_0+a_{01}m_1+\ldots+a_{07}m_7,$$

$$a_{10}m_0+a_{11}m_1+\ldots+a_{17}m_7$$

$$\ldots \qquad \ldots \qquad \ldots$$

$$a_{70}m_0+a_{71}m_1+\ldots+a_{77}m_7\ )\ \mathrm{mod}\ q$$

Let $(f_0,\ldots,f_7) = F(M)$.

We can calculate $m_0,\ldots,m_6$ and m_7 from $f_0,\ldots,f_6$ and f_7 as follows.

$$a_{00}m_0+a_{01}m_1+\ldots+a_{07}m_7\ \ \mathrm{mod}\ q=f_0$$

$$a_{10}m_0+a_{11}m_1+\ldots+a_{17}m_7\ \mathrm{mod}\ q=f_1$$

$$\ldots \qquad \ldots \qquad \ldots$$

$$a_{70}m_0+a_{71}m_1+\ldots+a_{77}m_7\ \mathrm{mod}\ q=f_7$$

where $\det(a_{ij})\neq 0\ \mathrm{mod}\ q$.

We solve the above simultaneous equation to obtain $m_0,\ldots,m_6$ and m_7.

Next let $F(G(X))\in \boldsymbol{O}[X]$ or $G(F(X))\in \boldsymbol{O}[X]$ be the composite function of $F(X)\in \boldsymbol{O}[X]$ and $G(X)\in \boldsymbol{O}[X]$

where

$$F(X)=A_1(A_2(\ldots(A_kX)\ldots)),$$

$$=(\ a_{00}x_0+a_{01}x_1+\ldots+a_{07}x_7,$$

$$a_{10}x_0+a_{11}x_1+\ldots+a_{17}x_7$$

$$\ldots \qquad \ldots \qquad \ldots$$

$$a_{70}x_0+a_{71}x_1+\ldots+a_{77}x_7\ )\ \mathrm{mod}\ q,$$

$A_i\in \boldsymbol{O}(i=1,\ldots,k)$ are the coefficients of $F(X)$, and

$$G(X)=B_1(B_2(\ldots(B_hX)\ldots),$$

$$=(\,b_{00}x_0+b_{01}x_1+\ldots+b_{07}x_7,$$

$$b_{10}x_0+b_{11}x_1+\ldots+b_{17}x_7$$

$$\ldots \qquad \ldots \qquad \ldots$$

$$b_{70}x_0+b_{71}x_1+\ldots+b_{77}x_7)\ \mathrm{mod}\ q$$

with $a_{ij} \in Fq(i,j=0,\ldots,7)$.

$B_i \in O(i=1,\ldots,h)$ is the coefficients of $G(X)$.

$F(G(X)) \in O[X]$ is obtained as follows.

$F(G(X))= A_1(A_2(\ldots(A_k(B_1(B_2(\ldots(B_hX)\ldots)\ \mathrm{mod}\ q,$

$=(\,a_{00}(b_{00}x_0+b_{01}x_1+\ldots+b_{07}x_7)+a_{01}(b_{10}x_0+b_{11}x_1+\ldots+b_{17}x_7)+\ldots+a_{07}(b_{70}x_0+b_{71}x_1+\ldots+b_{77}x_7),$

$a_{10}(b_{00}x_0+b_{01}x_1+\ldots+b_{07}x_7)+a_{11}(b_{10}x_0+b_{11}x_1+\ldots+b_{17}x_7)+\ldots+a_{17}(b_{70}x_0+b_{71}x_1+\ldots+b_{77}x_7),$

$$\ldots \qquad \ldots \qquad \ldots$$

$a_{70}(b_{00}x_0+b_{01}x_1+\ldots+b_{07}x_7)+a_{71}(b_{10}x_0+b_{11}x_1+\ldots+b_{17}x_7)+\ldots+a_{77}(b_{70}x_0+b_{71}x_1+\ldots+b_{77}x_7))\ \mathrm{mod}\ q,$

$=((a_{00}b_{00}+ a_{01}b_{10}+\ldots+ a_{07}b_{70})x_0+(\,a_{00}b_{01}+ a_{01}\,b_{11}+\ldots+a_{07}b_{71})x_1+\ldots+(a_{00}b_{07}+ a_{01}b_{17}+\ldots+ a_{07}b_{77})\,x_7,$

$(a_{10}b_{00}+ a_{11}b_{10}+\ldots+ a_{17}b_{70})x_0+(\,a_{10}b_{01}+ a_{11}\,b_{11}+\ldots+a_{17}b_{71})x_1+\ldots+(a_{10}b_{07}+ a_{11}b_{17}+\ldots+ a_{17}b_{77})\,x_7,$

$$\ldots \qquad \ldots \qquad \ldots$$

$(a_{70}b_{00}+ a_{71}b_{10}+\ldots+ a_{77}b_{70})x_0+(\,a_{70}b_{01}+ a_{71}\,b_{11}+\ldots+a_{77}b_{71})x_1+\ldots+(a_{70}b_{07}+ a_{71}b_{17}+\ldots+ a_{77}b_{77})\,x_7)$
$\mathrm{mod}\ q.$

Since multiplication on octonoin ring has the property of non-commutative and non-associative, we notice the following property of the polynomials on octonion ring.

Let

$$K(X):=C_1(C_2X)) \bmod q \in \boldsymbol{O}[X],$$

$$H(X,Y):= D_1(Y(D_2X) \bmod q \in \boldsymbol{O}[X,Y],$$

and

$$E(X,Y):=D_1(C_1(C_2(Y(D_2X)))) \bmod q \in \boldsymbol{O}[X,Y],$$

where

$C_1,C_2,D_1,D_2 \in \boldsymbol{O}$ are the coefficients and $X=(x_0,\ldots,x_7)$, $Y=(y_0,\ldots,y_7) \in \boldsymbol{O}[X]$ are symbols representing the full set of variables and D_1 has the inverse D_1^{-1} .

$$H(X, K(Y))= D_1(K(Y)(D_2X)) \bmod q$$

$$= D_1([C_1(C_2Y)](D_2X)) \bmod q.$$

When $X=Y=\mathbf{1}$, we obtain

$$H(X, K(Y))= D_1([C_1C_2]D_2) \bmod q,$$

$$E(X, Y) = D_1(C_1(C_2D_2)) \bmod q.$$

In general from non-associative property,

$$(C_1C_2)D_2 \neq C_1(C_2D_2) \bmod q.$$

Left-multiplying both sides by D_1 gives

$$D_1((C_1C_2)D_2) \neq D_1(C_1(C_2D_2)) \bmod q.$$

Then we have

$$H(X, K(Y)) \neq E(X,Y) \bmod q.$$

§4. Re-encryption scheme

Proxy re-encryption (PRE) schemes are cryptosystems which allow third parties (proxies) to alter a ciphertext which has been encrypted for one party, so that it may be decrypted by another.

Bob could designate a proxy to re-encrypt one of his messages that is to be sent to Chris. This generates a new key that Chris can use to decrypt the message. Now if Alice sends Chris a message that was encrypted under Bob's key, the proxy will alter the message, allowing Chris to decrypt it. This method allows for a number of applications such as e-mail forwarding, law-enforcement monitoring, and content distribution.

A weaker re-encryption scheme is one in which the proxy possesses both parties' keys simultaneously. One key decrypts a plaintext, while the other encrypts it. Since the goal of many proxy re-encryption schemes is to avoid revealing either of the keys or the underlying plaintext to the proxy, this method is not ideal.

In PRE, a user who has a secret key corresponding to his public key can decrypt a ciphertext encrypted with his public key. In addition the user can delegate his decryption capability to another user by providing a proxy with a re-encryption key and requesting the proxy to convert a ciphertext into a ciphertext that the delegatee can decrypt. Due to this delegation of decrypting capability, PRE can be used for various applications such as email forwarding, big data processing in cloud computing system and secure network file storage.

In the delegation process above, we must carefully consider a security property related to the proxy. Obviously the collusion of the proxy and a delegatee may result in the decryption of ciphertexts for a delegator if the ciphertexts are re-encrypted. This potential security threat from the collusion is inevitable because of the intrinsic delegation structure of a PRE scheme.

The secret keys of honest delegators must not be revealed from the collusion because these secret keys can be used for a variety of their own security tasks.

In chapter 4 a re-encryption scheme based on non-associative octonion ring is presented. This scheme does not need the proxy. This scheme is very useful for cloud computing systems where data of user are stored as the ciphertext. In addition the complexity required for the enciphering/deciphering in proposed scheme is enough small and speed of the enciphering/deciphering in proposed scheme is enough fast.

§5. Fully homomorphic enciphering/deciphering function (FHEDF)

FHEDF has the following property (in its simplest form). Ciphertexts c_i are deciphered to plaintexts m_i, i.e., Decrypt(c_i) = m_i, where the m_i's and c_i's are elements of some ring (with two operations, addition and multiplication). In fully homomorphic encryption (FHE) we have the expression such that

$$\text{Decrypt } (c_1 + c_2) = m_1 + m_2; \text{ Decrypt } (c_1{}^*c_2) = m_1{}^* \, m_2:$$

In other words, decryption is doubly homomorphic, i.e., homomorphic with respect to the two operations addition and multiplication.

Being fully homomorphic means that whenever f is a function composed of (finitely many) additions and multiplications in the ring, then

$$\text{Decrypt } (f(c_1,\ldots, c_t)) = f(m_1,\ldots,m_t):$$

If the cloud (or an adversary) can efficiently compute $f(c_1,\ldots, c_t)$ from ciphertexts $c_1,\ldots, c_t$, without learning any information about the corresponding plaintexts $m_1,\ldots,m_t$ then the system is efficient and secure.

Another requirement for FHEDF is that the ciphertext sizes remain bounded, independent of the function f; this is known as the "compact ciphertexts" requirement. (Depending on the filly homomorphic encryption systems, the messages and ciphertexts could in fact lie in different rings, and multiplication might be accomplished using a tensoring operation.)

Fully homomorphic encryption schemes belong to either public key cryptosystem (where the encryptor knows the decryptor's public key but not her private key) or symmetric key cryptosystem (where the encryptor and decryptor share a key that is used for both encryption and decryption). Fully homomorphic encryption scheme described in chapter 4 belongs to symmetric key cryptosystem. I will describe the new fully homomorphic encryption scheme to belong to public key cryptosystem in near future.

§6. Quantum computer

The principal of a quantum computer is based on quantum mechanical phenomena, such as superposition and entanglement. Quantum computers are different from von Neumann –type computers based on transistors. The basic principle behind quantum computation is that quantum properties can be used to represent data and perform operations on these data. The research is carried out in which quantum computational operations were executed on a very small number of qubits (quantum bits).

If large-scale quantum computers can be built, they will be able to solve certain problems much faster than any classical computer using the best currently known algorithms, for example, integer factorization using Shor's algorithm. Furthermore, there exist quantum algorithms, such as Simon's algorithm, which runs exponentially faster than any possible probabilistic classical algorithm.

It is said that the problem of factoring large integers, the problem of solving discrete logarithms and the problem of computing elliptic curve discrete logarithms are efficiently solved in a polynomial time by the quantum computers.

It is thought that the multivariate public key cryptosystem (MPKC) is immune from the attack of quantum computers because we probably need to solve the multivariate algebraic equations of high degree that is equal to solving the NP complete problem. Then it is thought that the cryptosystem proposed in chapter 4 is immune from the attacks by quantum computers.

§7. Gröbner basis attack

A Gröbner basis [1.1] is a set of multivariate polynomials that has desirable algorithmic properties. Every set of polynomials can be transformed into a Gröbner basis. A Gröbner basis is used to solve a system of polynomial. In the cryptography we can use Gröbner basis to break the public key cryptosystems based on the multivariate polynomials. It is what is called the Gröbner basis attack.

CHAPTER 2

PREVIOUS FULLY HOMOMORPHIC ENCRYPTION SCHEMES

The fully homomorphic encryption scheme has long been something of a Holy Grail for computer scientists. Craig Gentry's recent solution to the problem [0.8], while not efficient enough to be practical, was considered to be a major breakthrough. Then, much progress has been made in the direction of finding efficient **fully homomorphic encryption** (FHE) schemes.

A major application of FHE is to cloud computing system. User A can store his data in "the cloud", for example, on remote servers that he accesses via the Internet. The cloud has more storage capabilities and computing power than does user A, so when user A needs computations to be done on his data, user A would like those computations to be done by the cloud. However, user A doesn't trust the cloud. His data might be sensitive (for example, user A might be a hospital and the data might be patients' medical records), and user A would like the cloud to know as little as possible about his data, and about the results of the computations. So user A sends encrypted data to the cloud, which can perform arithmetic operations on it without learning anything about the original raw data, by performing operations on the encrypted data.

Here for reader's understanding we show the survey of the fully homomorphic encryption below.

The utility of fully homomorphic encryption has been long recognized. The problem of constructing such a scheme was first proposed within a year of the development of RSA [2.1]. For more than 30 years, it was unclear whether fully homomorphic encryption was possible. During this period, the best result was the Boneh-Goh-Nissim cryptosystem which supports evaluation of an unlimited number of addition operations but at most one multiplication.

Craig Gentry [0.9] using lattice-based cryptosystem showed the first fully homomorphic encryption scheme as announced by IBM on June 25, 2009 [2.2][2.3]. His scheme supports evaluations of arbitrary depth circuits. His construction starts from a somewhat homomorphic encryption scheme using ideal lattices that is limited to evaluating low-degree polynomials over encrypted data. (It is limited because each ciphertext is noisy in some sense, and this noise grows as one adds and multiplies ciphertexts, until ultimately the noise makes the resulting ciphertext indecipherable.) He then shows how to modify this scheme to make it bootstrappable—in particular, he shows that by modifying the somewhat homomorphic scheme slightly, it can actually evaluate its own decryption circuit, a self-referential property. Finally, he shows that any bootstrappable somewhat homomorphic encryption scheme can be converted into a fully homomorphic encryption through a recursive self-embedding.

However, the scheme is impractical for many applications, because ciphertext size and computation time increase sharply as one increases the security level. (Let k be the security parameter.) To obtain 2^k security against known attacks, the computation time and ciphertext size are high-degree polynomials in k.

In 2010, Stehle and Steinfeld reduced the dependence on k substantially [2.4]. They presented optimizations that permit the computation to be only quasi-$k^{3.5}$ per boolean gate of the function being evaluated.

Gentry's Ph.D. thesis [2.5] provides additional details. Gentry also published a high-level overview of the van Dijk et al. construction (described below) in the March 2010 issue of Communications of the ACM [2.6].

In 2009, Marten van Dijk, Craig Gentry, Shai Halevi and Vinod Vaikuntanathan presented a second fully homomorphic encryption scheme [2.7], which uses many of the tools of Gentry's construction, but which does not require ideal lattices. Instead, they show that the somewhat homomorphic component of Gentry's ideal lattice-based scheme can be replaced with a very simple somewhat homomorphic scheme that uses integers. The scheme is therefore conceptually simpler than Gentry's ideal lattice scheme, but has similar properties with regards to homomorphic operations and efficiency. The somewhat homomorphic component in the work of van Dijk et al. is similar to an encryption scheme proposed by Levieil and Naccache in 2008, and also to one that was proposed by Bram Cohen in 1998[2.8]. Cohen's method is not even additively homomorphic, however. The Levieil-Naccache scheme is additively homomorphic, and can be modified to support also a small number of multiplications.

In 2011, Coron, Naccache and Tibouchi proposed a technique allowing to reduce the public-key size $O(\lambda^{10})$ of the van Dijk et al. scheme to $O(\lambda^7)$ [2.9].

In April 2013 the HElib was released, via GitHub, to the open source community which "implements the Brakerski-Gentry- Vaikuntanathan (BGV) homomorphic encryption scheme, along with many optimizations to make homomorphic evaluation runs faster" [2.10].

Recently, Nuida and Kurosawa proposed (batch) fully homomorphic encryption over integers [2.11].

The fully homomorphic encryptions described above have the large complexity for enciphering
/deciphering. In chapter 4, I describe the fully homomorphic encryption scheme based on the octonion ring over Fq which have the non-associative and non-commutative property. That is, the scheme has additively homomorphic and multiplicative homomorphic property.

CHAPTER 3

EXAMPLES OF FULLY HOMOMORPHIC ENCIPHERING

FUNCTION ON OCTONION RING O

In this chapter I describe two example of fully homomorphic enciphering functions which are adopted in chapter 4.

§1. Example 1

Let q be a prime more than 2.

Let $M_i = (m_{i0}, m_{i1}, \ldots, m_{i7}) \in O$ be the plaintext to be encrypted .(i=1,2)

Let $X = (x_0, \ldots, x_7) \in O[X]$ be a variable.

Let $E(M_i, X)$ be a enciphering function of user A.

Let $E(M_i, X) \in O[X]$ be the ciphertext. (i=1,2)

$A_i \in O$ is selected randomly such that A_i^{-1} exists (i=1,...,k) which is the secret keys of user A.

$E(M_i, X)$ is defined as follows.

$$E(M_i, X) := A_1(\ldots(A_k(M_i(A_k^{-1}(\ldots(A_1^{-1}X)\ldots)) \bmod q \in O[X] \ (i=1,2),$$

[Addition of $E(M_1, X)$ and $E(M_2, X)$]

$$E(M_1, X) \pm E(M_2, X) \bmod q$$

$$= A_1(\ldots(A_k(M_1(A_k^{-1}(\ldots(A_1^{-1}X)\ldots)\ldots) + A_1(\ldots(A_k(M_2(A_k^{-1}(\ldots(A_1^{-1}X)\ldots)\ldots) \bmod q$$

$$= A_1(\ldots(A_k([M_1 \pm M_2](A_k^{-1}(\ldots(A_1^{-1}X)\ldots)\ldots) \bmod q.$$

That is,

$$E(M_1, X) \pm E(M_2, X) = E(M_1 \pm M_2, X) \bmod q.$$

[Multiplication of $E(M_1, X)$ and $E(M_2, X)$]

$$E(M_1, E(M_2, X)) \bmod q$$

$$= A_1(\ldots(A_k(M_1(A_k^{-1}(\ldots(A_1^{-1}(A_1(\ldots(A_k(M_2(A_k^{-1}(\ldots(A_1^{-1}X)\ldots)\ldots)\ldots)\ldots) \bmod q$$

$$= A_1(\ldots(A_k(M_1(M_2(A_k^{-1}(\ldots(A_1^{-1}X)\ldots) \quad \bmod q$$

We can obtain the plaintext $(M_1 M_2)$ by deciphering as follws.

$$D: = A_k^{-1}(\ldots(A_1^{-1}(E(M_1, E\,(M_2,X))\ldots) \text{ at } X = A_1(\ldots(A_k\mathbf{1})\ldots) \bmod q$$

$$= A_k^{-1}(\ldots(A_1^{-1}(A_1(\ldots(A_k(M_1\,(M_2\,(A_k^{-1}\,(\ldots(A_1{}^{-1}(A_1(\ldots(A_k\mathbf{1})\ldots))\ldots) \bmod q$$

$$= M_1\,(M_2\,(\mathbf{1})) \bmod q$$

$$= M_1 M_2 \bmod q.$$

§2. Example 2

We also use the same definition of q, A_i, $X = (x_0, \ldots, x_7)$ and $E(M_i, X)$ as example 1.

And we select the element $B = (b_0, \ldots, b_7) \in O$ such that,

$$L_B := |B|^2 = b_0^2 + b_1^2 + \ldots + b_7^2 \bmod q = 0.$$

Let S_B be the partial set of O such that

$$S_B := \{ B = (b_0, \ldots, b_7) \in O \mid |B|^2 = b_0^2 + b_1^2 + \ldots + b_7^2 \bmod q = 0 \}.$$

Let $u_i \in Fq$ be the plaintext.($i=1, 2$)
Let $v_i \in Fq$ be the random number. ($i=1, 2$)
$M_i \in O$ is defined as follows. ($i=1, 2$)

$$M_1 = u_1\mathbf{1} + v_1 B \bmod q \in O,$$

$$M_2 = u_2\mathbf{1} + v_2 B \bmod q \in O.$$

$E(M_1, E\,(M_2, X)) \bmod q$

$$= A_1(\ldots(A_k(M_1(M_2(A_k^{-1}\,(\ldots(A_1{}^{-1}X)\ldots) \bmod q$$

$$= A_1(\ldots(A_k(\,[u_1\mathbf{1} + v_1 B][u_2\mathbf{1} + v_2 B](\,A_k^{-1}\,(\ldots(A_1{}^{-1}X)\ldots) \bmod q$$

$$= A_1(\ldots(A_k(\,[u_1\mathbf{1}][u_2\mathbf{1} + v_2 B](\,A_k^{-1}\,(\ldots(A_1{}^{-1}X)\ldots) + A_1(\ldots(A_k(\,[v_1 B][u_2\mathbf{1} + v_2 B](\,A_k^{-1}\,(\ldots(A_1{}^{-1}X)\ldots) \bmod q$$

$$= A_1(\ldots(A_k[u_1\mathbf{1}][u_2\mathbf{1}](\,A_k^{-1}\,(\ldots(A_1{}^{-1}X)\ldots) + A_1(\ldots(A_k[u_1\mathbf{1}][v_2 B](\,A_k^{-1}\,(\ldots(A_1{}^{-1}X)\ldots) \bmod q$$

$$+ A_1(\ldots(A_k[v_1 B][u_2\mathbf{1}](\,A_k^{-1}\,(\ldots(A_1{}^{-1}X)\ldots) + A_1(\ldots(A_k(\,[v_1 B][v_2 B](\,A_k^{-1}\,(\ldots(A_1{}^{-1}X)\ldots) \bmod q$$

$$= A_1(\ldots(A_k(\,[u_1 u_2\mathbf{1}](A_k^{-1}\,(\ldots(A_1{}^{-1}X)\ldots) + A_1(\ldots(A_k(\,[u_1 v_2 B](A_k^{-1}\,(\ldots(A_1{}^{-1}X)\ldots) \bmod q$$

$$+ A_1(\ldots(A_k([v_1u_2B](A_k^{-1}(\ldots(A_1^{-1}X)\ldots))+ A_1(\ldots(A_k([v_1v_2BB](A_k^{-1}(\ldots(A_1^{-1}X)\ldots) \bmod q$$

$$= A_1(\ldots(A_k([u_1u_21 + v_1u_2B + u_1v_2B + v_1v_2BB](A_k^{-1}(\ldots(A_1^{-1}X)\ldots) \bmod q$$

$$= A_1(\ldots(A_k([u_11u_21 + v_1 B u_21 + u_11v_2B + v_1Bv_2B](A_k^{-1}(\ldots(A_1^{-1}X)\ldots) \bmod q$$

$$= A_1(\ldots(A_k([u_11(u_21 + v_2B) + v_1 B(u_21 + v_2B)](A_k^{-1}(\ldots(A_1^{-1}X)\ldots) \bmod q$$

$$= A_1(\ldots(A_k([(u_11 + v_1B)(u_21 + v_2B)](A_k^{-1}(\ldots(A_1^{-1}X)\ldots) \bmod q$$

$$= A_1(\ldots(A_k([M_1M_2](A_k^{-1}(\ldots(A_1^{-1}X)\ldots) \bmod q$$

$$= E(M_1M_2, X) \bmod q.$$

In chapter 4 the fully homomorphic encryption scheme using the above property of example 1 is proposed.

CHAPTER 4

PROPOSED FULLY HOMOMORPHIC ENCRYPTION

SUMMARY: Gentry's bootstrapping technique is still the only known method of obtaining fully homomorphic encryption. I propose a new fully homomorphic encryption scheme on non-associative octonion ring over finite field without bootstrapping technique. The security of the proposed fully homomorphic encryption scheme is based on computational difficulty to solve the multivariate algebraic equations of high degree while the almost all multivariate cryptosystems [0.5], [4.1],[4.2],[4.3],[4.4],[4.5] proposed until now are based on the quadratic equations avoiding the explosion of the coefficients. Because proposed fully homomorphic encryption scheme is based on multivariate algebraic equations with high degree or too many variables, it is against the Gröbner basis [1.1] attack, the differential attack, rank attack and so on.

The key size of this system and complexity for enciphering/deciphering become to be small enough to handle.

keywords: fully homomorphic encryption, multivariate algebraic equation, Gröbner basis, octonion

§1. Introduction

A cryptosystem which supports both addition and multiplication (thereby preserving the ring structure of the plaintexts) is known as fully homomorphic encryption (FHE) and is very powerful. Using such a scheme, any circuit can be homomorphically evaluated, effectively allowing the construction of programs which may be run on encryptions of their inputs to produce an encryption of their output. Since such a program never decrypts its input, it can be run by an untrusted party without revealing its inputs and internal state. The existence of an efficient and fully homomorphic cryptosystem would have great practical implications in the outsourcing of private computations, for instance, in the context of cloud computing.

With homomorphic encryption, a company could encrypt its entire database of e-mails and upload it to a cloud. Then it could use the cloud-stored data as desired—for example, to calculate the stochastic value of stored data. The results would be downloaded and decrypted without ever exposing the details of a single e-mail.

In 2009 Gentry, an IBM researcher, has created a homomorphic encryption scheme that makes it possible to encrypt the data in such a way that performing a mathematical operation on the encrypted information and then decrypting the result produces the same answer as performing an analogous operation on the unencrypted data.

But in Gentry's scheme a task like finding a piece of text in an e-mail requires chaining together thousands of basic operations. His solution was to use a second layer of encryption, essentially to protect intermediate results when the system broke down and needed to be reset.

In this paper I propose a fully homomorphic encryption scheme on non-associative octonion ring over finite field which is based on computational difficulty to solve the multivariate algebraic equations of high degree while the almost all multivariate cryptosystems [4.2],[4.3],[4.4],[4.5] proposed until now are based on the quadratic equations avoiding the explosion of the coefficients. Our scheme is against the Gröbner basis [1.1] attack, the differential attack, rank attack and so on.

Organization of this chapter is as follows. In Sec.2 preliminaries for octonion operation are described. In Sec.3 we construct proposed fully homomorphic encryption scheme. In Sec.4 the procedure for proposed fully homomorphic encryption scheme is described. In Sec.5 re-encryption scheme is described. In Sec.6 we analyse proposed scheme to show that proposed scheme is immune from the Gröbner basis attacks by calculating the complexity to obtain the Gröbner basis for the multivariate algebraic equations. In Sec.7 we describe the size of the parameters and the complexity for enciphering and deciphering. In Sec.8 we describe conclusion of chapter 4.

§2. Preliminaries for octonion operation

In this section we describe the operations on octonion ring and properties of octonion ring.

§2.1 Multiplication and addition on the octonion ring O

Let q be a fixed modulus to be as large prime as $O(2^{10})$.
Let O be the octonion [0.9] ring over a finite field Fq.

$$O=\{(a_0,a_1,...,a_7) \mid a_j \in Fq \ (j=0,1,...,7)\} \tag{4.1}$$

We define the multiplication and addition of $A,B \in O$ as follows.

$$A=(a_0,a_1,...,a_7), \ a_j \in Fq \ (j=0,1,...,7), \tag{4.2}$$

$$B=(b_0,b_1,\ldots,b_7),\ b_j \in Fq\ (j=0,1,\ldots,7). \tag{4.3}$$

$AB \bmod q$

$$
\begin{aligned}
=\ & (a_0b_0 - a_1b_1 - a_2b_2 - a_3b_3 - a_4b_4 - a_5b_5 - a_6b_6 - a_7b_7 \bmod q, \\
& a_0b_1 + a_1b_0 + a_2b_4 + a_3b_7 - a_4b_2 + a_5b_6 - a_6b_5 - a_7b_3 \bmod q, \\
& a_0b_2 - a_1b_4 + a_2b_0 + a_3b_5 + a_4b_1 - a_5b_3 + a_6b_7 - a_7b_6 \bmod q, \\
& a_0b_3 - a_1b_7 - a_2b_5 + a_3b_0 + a_4b_6 + a_5b_2 - a_6b_4 + a_7b_1 \bmod q, \\
& a_0b_4 + a_1b_2 - a_2b_1 - a_3b_6 + a_4b_0 + a_5b_7 + a_6b_3 - a_7b_5 \bmod q, \\
& a_0b_5 - a_1b_6 + a_2b_3 - a_3b_2 - a_4b_7 + a_5b_0 + a_6b_1 + a_7b_4 \bmod q, \\
& a_0b_6 + a_1b_5 - a_2b_7 + a_3b_4 - a_4b_3 - a_5b_1 + a_6b_0 + a_7b_2 \bmod q, \\
& a_0b_7 + a_1b_3 + a_2b_6 - a_3b_1 + a_4b_5 - a_5b_4 - a_6b_2 + a_7b_0 \bmod q) \tag{4.4}
\end{aligned}
$$

$A+B \bmod q$

$$
\begin{aligned}
=(& a_0+b_0 \bmod q,\ a_1+b_1 \bmod q,\ a_2+b_2 \bmod q,\ a_3+b_3 \bmod q, \\
& a_4+b_4 \bmod q,\ a_5+b_5 \bmod q,\ a_6+b_6 \bmod q,\ a_7+b_7 \bmod q). \tag{4.5}
\end{aligned}
$$

Let

$$|A|^2 = a_0^2 + a_1^2 + \ldots + a_7^2 \bmod q. \tag{4.6}$$

If $|A|^2 \neq 0 \bmod q$, we can have A^{-1}, the inverse of A by using the algorithm **Octinv**(A) such that

$$A^{-1} = (a_0/|A|^2 \bmod q,\ -a_1/|A|^2 \bmod q,\ldots,\ -a_7/|A|^2 \bmod q) \leftarrow \textbf{Octinv}(A)\ldots(4.7)$$

Here details of the algorithm **Octinv**(A) are omitted and can be looked up in the **Appendix A.**

§2.2 Order of the element in O

In this section we describe the order "J" of the element "A" in octonion ring, that is,

$$A^{J+1}=A \bmod q.$$

Theorem 4.1.

Let $A:=(a_{10},a_{11},\ldots,a_{17}) \in O,\ a_{1j} \in Fq\quad (j=0,1,\ldots,7).$

Let $(a_{n0},a_{n1},\ldots,a_{n7}) := A^n \in O,\ a_{nj} \in Fq\quad (n=1,2,\ldots;j=0,1,\ldots,7).$

a_{00} , a_{nj}'s($n=1,2,...;j=0,1,...$) and b_n's($n=0,1,...$) satisfy the equations such that

$$N:= a_{11}{}^2+...+a_{17}{}^2 \mod q$$

$$a_{00}:=1, \; b_0:=0, \; b_1:=1,$$

$$a_{n0}= a_{n-1,0}\,a_{10} - b_{n-1}N \mod q \,,(n=1,2,...), \tag{4.8}$$

$$b_n = a_{n-1,0}+ b_{n-1}a_{10} \mod q \,,(n=1,2,...), \tag{4.9}$$

$$a_{nj}= b_n a_{1j} \mod q \,,(n=1,2,...;j=1,2,...,7) . \tag{4.10}$$

(*Proof.*)

Here proof is omitted and can be looked up in the **Appendix B**.

Theorem 4.2.

For an element $A=(a_{10},a_{11},...,a_{17})\in O$,

$$A^{J+1}=A \mod q,$$

where

$$J= LCM \{q^2\text{-}1, \; q\text{-}1\}=q^2\text{-}1,$$

$$N:=a_{11}{}^2+ a_{12}{}^2+...+a_{17}{}^2 \neq 0 \mod q.$$

(*Proof.*)

Here proof is omitted and can be looked up in the **Appendix C**.

§2.3. Property of multiplication over octonion ring O

A,B,C etc.$\in O$ satisfy the following formulae in general where A,B and C have the inverse A^{-1} ,B^{-1} and C^{-1} mod q.

1) Non-commutative

$$AB \neq BA \mod q.$$

2) Non-associative

$$A(BC) \neq (AB)C \mod q.$$

3) Alternative

$$(AA)B=A(AB) \mod q, \tag{4.11}$$

$$A(BB)=(AB)B \quad \mod q, \tag{4.12}$$

$$(AB)A=A(BA) \quad \mod q. \tag{4.13}$$

4) Moufang's formulae [6],

$$C(A(CB))=((CA)C)B \quad \mod q, \tag{4.14}$$

$$A(C(BC))=((AC)B)C \quad \mod q, \tag{4.15}$$

$$(CA)(BC)=(C(AB))C \quad \mod q, \tag{4.16}$$

$$(CA)(BC)=C((AB)C) \quad \mod q. \tag{4.17}$$

5) For positive integers n,m, we have

$$(AB)B^n =((AB)B^{n-1})B=A(B(B^{n-1}B))=AB^{n+1} \quad \mod q, \tag{4.18}$$

$$(AB^n)B =((AB)B^{n-1})B=A(B(B^{n-1}B))=AB^{n+1} \quad \mod q, \tag{4.19}$$

$$B^n (BA) =B(B^{n-1}(BA))= ((BB^{n-1})B)A=B^{n+1}A \quad \mod q, \tag{4.20}$$

$$B(B^n A)=B(B^{n-1}(BA))= ((BB^{n-1})B)A=B^{n+1}A \quad \mod q. \tag{4.21}$$

From (4.12) and (4.19), we have

$$[(AB^n)B]B =[AB^{n+1}]B \quad \mod q,$$

$$(AB^n)(BB) =[(AB^n)B]B =[AB^{n+1}]B= AB^{n+2} \mod q,$$

$$(AB^n)B^2= AB^{n+2} \mod q,$$

$$\cdots \quad \cdots$$

$$(AB^n)B^m= AB^{n+m} \mod q.$$

In the same way we have

$$B^m(B^n A)= B^{n+m}A \quad \mod q.$$

6) **Lemma 4.1.**

$$A(B((AB)^n))=(AB)^{n+1} \quad \mod q,$$

$$(((AB)^n)A)B =(AB)^{n+1} \mod q.$$

where n is a positive integer and B has the inverse B^{-1}.

(*Proof.*)

From (4.14) we have

$$B(A(B((AB)^n)=((BA)B)(AB)^n=(B(AB))(AB)^n=B(AB)^{n+1} \mod q.$$

Then

$$B^{-1}(B(A(B(AB)^n))= B^{-1}(B \ (AB)^{n+1}) \mod q,$$

$$A(B(AB)^n)= (AB)^{n+1} \mod q.$$

In the same way we have

$$(((AB)^n)A)B=(AB)^{n+1} \mod q. \qquad\qquad \text{q.e.d.}$$

7) **Lemma 4.2.**

$$A^{-1}(AB)= B \mod q,$$

$$(BA)A^{-1}= B \mod q .$$

(*Proof*:)

Here proof is omitted and can be looked up in the **Appendix D**.

8) **Lemma 4.3.**

$$A(BA^{-1})= (AB)A^{-1} \mod q.$$

(*Proof*:)

From (4.17) we substitute A^{-1} to C, we have

$$(A^{-1}A)(B \ A^{-1})= A^{-1} ((AB) \ A^{-1}) \mod q,$$

$$(B \ A^{-1})= A^{-1} ((AB) \ A^{-1}) \mod q.$$

We multiply A from left side ,

$$A(B \ A^{-1})= A(A^{-1} ((AB) \ A^{-1}))= (AB) \ A^{-1} \mod q. \qquad\qquad \text{q.e.d.}$$

We can express $A(BA^{-1})$, $(AB)A^{-1}$ such that

$$ABA^{-1}.$$

9) From (4.13) and Lemma 4.2 we have

$$A^{-1}((A(BA^{-1}))A)= A^{-1}(A((BA^{-1})A))= (BA^{-1})A=B \mod q,$$

$$(A^{-1}((AB)A^{-1}))A=((A^{-1}(AB))A^{-1})A= A^{-1}(AB)=B \bmod q.$$

10) **Lemma 4.4.**

$$(BA^{-1})(AB)=B^2 \bmod q.$$

(*Proof:*)

From (4.17),

$$(BA^{-1})(AB)=B((A^{-1}A)B)=B^2 \quad \bmod q. \qquad\qquad \text{q.e.d.}$$

11) **Lemma 4.5.**

$$(ABA^{-1})(ABA^{-1})= AB^2A^{-1} \bmod q.$$

(*Proof:*)

From (4.17),

$$(ABA^{-1})(ABA^{-1}) \quad \bmod q$$

$$=[A^{-1} (A^2(BA^{-1}))][(AB)A^{-1}]= A^{-1} \{[(A^2(BA^{-1}))(AB)]A^{-1}\} \quad \bmod q$$

$$= A^{-1} \{[(A(A(BA^{-1})))(AB)]A^{-1}\} \quad \bmod q$$

$$= A^{-1} \{[(A((AB)A^{-1}))(AB)]A^{-1}\} \quad \bmod q$$

$$= A^{-1} \{[(A(AB))A^{-1}))(AB)]A^{-1}\} \quad \bmod q.$$

We apply (4.15) to inside of [.],

$$= A^{-1} \{[(A((AB)(A^{-1}(AB))))]A^{-1}\} \quad \bmod q$$

$$= A^{-1} \{[(A((AB)B))]A^{-1}\} \quad \bmod q$$

$$= A^{-1} \{[A(A(BB))]A^{-1}\} \quad \bmod q$$

$$=\{ A^{-1} [A(A(BB))]\}A^{-1} \quad \bmod q$$

$$=(A(BB))A^{-1} \quad \bmod q$$

$$=AB^2A^{-1} \bmod q. \qquad\qquad \text{q.e.d.}$$

12) **Lemma 4.6.**

$$(AB^mA^{-1})(AB^nA^{-1})= AB^{m+n}A^{-1} \quad \bmod q.$$

(*Proof:*)

From (4.16),

$$[A^{-1}(A^2(B^mA^{-1}))][(AB^n)A^{-1}]= \{A^{-1}[(A^2(B^mA^{-1}))(AB^n)]\}A^{-1} \mod q$$

$$= A^{-1}\{[(A(A(B^mA^{-1}))(AB^n)]A^{-1}\} \mod q$$

$$= A^{-1}\{[(A((AB^m)A^{-1}))(AB^n)]A^{-1}\} \mod q$$

$$= A^{-1}\{[((A(AB^m))A^{-1}))(AB^n)]A^{-1}\} \mod q$$

$$= A^{-1}\{[((A^2B^m)A^{-1}))(AB^n)]A^{-1}\} \mod q.$$

We apply (4.15) to inside of { . },

$$= A^{-1}\{(A^2B^m)[A^{-1}((AB^n)A^{-1})]\} \mod q$$

$$= A^{-1}\{(A^2B^m)[A^{-1}(A(B^nA^{-1}))]\} \mod q$$

$$= A^{-1}\{(A^2B^m)(B^nA^{-1})\} \mod q$$

$$= A^{-1}\{(A^{-1}(A^3B^m))(B^nA^{-1})\} \mod q.$$

We apply (4.17) to inside of { . },

$$= A^{-1}\{A^{-1}([(A^3B^m)B^n]A^{-1})]\} \mod q$$

$$= A^{-1}\{A^{-1}((A^3B^{m+n})A^{-1})\} \mod q$$

$$= A^{-1}\{(A^{-1}(A^3B^{m+n}))A^{-1}\} \mod q$$

$$= A^{-1}\{(A^2B^{m+n})A^{-1}\} \mod q$$

$$= \{A^{-1}(A^2B^{m+n}))\}A^{-1} \mod q$$

$$= (AB^{m+n})A^{-1} \mod q$$

$$= AB^{m+n}A^{-1} \mod q. \qquad\qquad \text{q.e.d}$$

13) $A \in O$ satisfies the following theorem.

Theorem 4.3.

$$A^2 = w\mathbf{1} + vA \mod q,$$

where

$$\exists w, v \in Fq,$$

$$\mathbf{1} = (1,0,0,0,0,0,0,0) \in O,$$

$$A = (a_0, a_1, \ldots, a_7) \in O.$$

(*Proof:*)

$A^2 \bmod q$

$=(\quad a_0a_0 - a_1a_1 - a_2a_2 - a_3a_3 - a_4a_4 - a_5a_5 - a_6a_6 - a_7a_7 \bmod q,$

$a_0a_1 + a_1a_0 + a_2a_4 + a_3a_7 - a_4a_2 + a_5a_6 - a_6a_5 - a_7a_3 \bmod q,$

$a_0a_2 - a_1a_4 + a_2a_0 + a_3a_5 + a_4a_1 - a_5a_3 + a_6a_7 - a_7a_6 \bmod q,$

$a_0a_3 - a_1a_7 - a_2a_5 + a_3a_0 + a_4a_6 + a_5a_2 - a_6a_4 + a_7a_1 \bmod q,$

$a_0a_4 + a_1a_2 - a_2a_1 - a_3a_6 + a_4a_0 + a_5a_7 + a_6a_3 - a_7a_5 \bmod q,$

$a_0a_5 - a_1a_6 + a_2a_3 - a_3a_2 - a_4a_7 + a_5a_0 + a_6a_1 + a_7a_4 \bmod q,$

$a_0a_6 + a_1a_5 - a_2a_7 + a_3a_4 - a_4a_3 - a_5a_1 + a_6a_0 + a_7a_2 \bmod q,$

$a_0a_7 + a_1a_3 + a_2a_6 - a_3a_1 + a_4a_5 - a_5a_4 - a_6a_2 + a_7a_0 \bmod q)$

$=(2a_0^2 - L \bmod q,\ 2a_0a_1 \bmod q,\ 2a_0a_2 \bmod q,\ 2a_0a_3 \bmod q,\ 2a_0a_4 \bmod q,\ 2a_0a_5 \bmod q,$

$2a_0a_6 \bmod q,\ 2a_0a_7 \bmod q)$

where

$$L = a_0^2 + a_1^2 + a_2^2 + a_3^2 + a_4^2 + a_5^2 + a_6^2 + a_7^2 \bmod q.$$

Now we try to obtain $u,\ v \in Fq$ that satisfy $A^2 = w\mathbf{1} + vA \bmod q$.

$$w\mathbf{1} + vA = w(1,0,0,0,0,0,0,0) + v(a_0, a_1, ..., a_7) \bmod q,$$

$A^2 = (2a_0^2 - L \bmod q,\ 2a_0a_1 \bmod q,\ 2a_0a_2 \bmod q,\ 2a_0a_3 \bmod q,\ 2a_0a_4 \bmod q,\ 2\ a_0a_5 \bmod$

$q,$

$2a_0a_6 \bmod q,\ 2\ a_0a_7 \bmod q).$

Then we have

$$A^2 = w\mathbf{1} + vA = -L\mathbf{1} + 2\ a_0A \bmod q,$$

$$w = -L \bmod q,$$

$$v = 2a_0 \bmod q. \qquad\qquad \text{q.e.d.}$$

14) **Theorem 4.4.**

$$A^h = w_h\mathbf{1} + v_hA \bmod q$$

where h is an integer and $w_h, v_h \in Fq$.

(*Proof:*)

From Theorem 4.3

$$A^2=w_2\mathbf{1}+v_2A=-L\mathbf{1}+2a_0A \text{ mod } q.$$

If we can express A^h such that

$$A^h=w_h\mathbf{1}+v_hA \text{ mod } q \in O, \ w_h,v_h \in Fq,$$

Then

$$A^{h+1}=(w_h\mathbf{1}+v_hA)A \text{ mod } q$$

$$=w_hA+v_h(-L\mathbf{1}+2\,a_0A\,) \text{ mod } q$$

$$=-L\,v_h\mathbf{1}+(\,w_h+2a_0\,v_h)A \text{ mod } q.$$

We have

$$w_{h+1}=-L\,v_h \text{ mod } q \in Fq,$$

$$v_{h+1}=w_h+2a_0v_h \ \text{ mod } q \in Fq. \hspace{2cm} \text{q.e.d.}$$

15) Theorem 4.5.

$D \in O$ does not exist that satisfies the following equation.

$$B(AX)=DX \text{ mod } q,$$

where $B,A,D \in O$, and X is a variable.

(*Proof:*)

When $X=\mathbf{1}$, we have

$$BA=D \text{ mod } q.$$

Then

$$B(AX)=(BA)X \text{ mod } q.$$

We can select $C \in O$ that satisfies

$$B(AC)\neq(BA)C \text{ mod } q \hspace{2cm} (4.22)$$

We substitute $C \in O$ to X to obtain

$$B(AC)=(BA)C. \text{ mod } q \hspace{2cm} (4.23)$$

(4.23) is contradictory to (4.22). $\hspace{3cm}$ q.e.d.

16) **Theorem 4.6.**

$D \in O$ does not exist that satisfies the following equation.

$$C(B(AX))=DX \bmod q \qquad (4.24)$$

where $C,B,A,D \in O$, C has inverse $C^{-1} \bmod q$ and X is a variable.

B,A,C are non-associative, that is,

$$B(AC) \neq (BA)C \bmod q. \qquad (4.25)$$

(*Proof.*)

If D exists, we have at $X=1$

$$C(BA)=D \bmod q.$$

Then

$$C(B(AX))=(C(BA))X \bmod q.$$

We substitute C to X to obtain

$$C(B(AC))=(C(BA))C \bmod q.$$

From (4.13)

$$C(B(AC))=(C(BA))C=C((BA)C) \bmod q$$

Multiplying C^{-1} from left side ,

$$B(AC)=(BA)C \bmod q \qquad (4.26)$$

(4.26) is contradictory to (4.25). q.e.d.

17) **Theorem 4.7**

D and $E \in O$ do not exist that satisfy the following equation.

$$C(B(AX))= E (DX) \bmod q$$

where C,B,A,D and $E \in O$ have inverse and X is a variable.

A,B,C are non-associative, that is,

$$C(BA) \neq (CB)A \bmod q. \qquad (4.27)$$

(*Proof.*)

If D and E exist, we have at $X=1$

$$C(BA)=ED \text{ mod} \qquad (4.28)$$

We have at $X=(ED)^{-1}=D^{-1}E^{-1} \text{ mod } q.$

$$C(B(A(D^{-1}E^{-1})))= E\ (D(D^{-1}E^{-1})) \text{ mod } q=1$$

$$(C(B(A(D^{-1}E^{-1})))^{-1} \text{ mod } q=1$$

$$((ED)A^{-1})B^{-1})C^{-1} \text{ mod } q=1$$

$$ED =(CB)A \text{ mod} \qquad (4.29)$$

From (4.28) and (4.29) we have

$$C(BA) =(CB)A \text{ mod} \qquad (4.30)$$

(4.30) is contradictory to (4.27). q.e.d.

18) **Theorem 4.8.**

$D \in O$ does not exist that satisfies the following equation.

$$A(B(A^{-1}X))=DX \text{ mod } q$$

where $B,A,D \in O$, A has inverse $A^{-1} \text{ mod } q$ and X is a variable.

(*Proof:*)

If D exists, we have at $X=1$

$$A(BA^{-1})=D \text{ mod } q.$$

Then

$$A\ (B(A^{-1}X))=(A(BA^{-1}))X \text{ mod } q \qquad (4.31)$$

We can select $C \in O$ such that

$$(BA^{-1})(CA^2) \ \neq \ (BA^{-1})C)A^2 \text{ mod } q. \qquad (4.32)$$

That is, (BA^{-1}), C and A^2 are non-associative.

Substituing $X=CA$ in (4.31), we have

$$A\ (B(A^{-1}(CA)))=(A(BA^{-1}))(CA) \text{ mod } q,$$

From Lemma 4.3.

$$A\left(B\left((A^{-1}C)A\right)\right)=(A(BA^{-1}))(CA) \bmod q,$$

From (4.17)

$$A\left(B\left((A^{-1}C)A\right)\right)=A\left([(BA^{-1})C]A\right) \bmod q.$$

Multiply A^{-1} from left side we have

$$B\left((A^{-1}C)A\right)=((BA^{-1})C)A \bmod q,$$

From Lemma 4.3.

$$B\left(A^{-1}(CA)\right)=((BA^{-1})C)A \bmod q,$$

Transforming CA to $((CA^2)A^{-1})$, we have

$$B\left(A^{-1}((CA^2)A^{-1})\right)=((BA^{-1})C)A \bmod q.$$

From (4.15) we have

$$((BA^{-1})(CA^2))A^{-1}=((BA^{-1})C)A \bmod q.$$

Multiply A from right side we have

$$((BA^{-1})(CA^2)=((BA^{-1})C)A^2 \bmod q. \tag{4.33}$$

(4.33) is contradictory to (4.32).   q.e.d.

§3. Concept of proposed fully homomorphic encryption scheme

Homomorphic encryption is a form of encryption which allows specific types of computations to be carried out on ciphertext and obtain an encrypted result which decrypted matches the result of operations performed on the plaintext. For instance, one person could add two encrypted numbers and then another person could decrypt the result, without either of them being able to find the value of the individual numbers.

§3.1 Definition of homomorphic encryption

A homomorphic encryption scheme HE := (**KeyGen; Enc; Dec; Eval**) is a quadruple of PPT (Probabilistic polynomial time) algorithms.

In this work, the message space M of the encryption schemes will be octonion ring, and the functions to be evaluated will be represented as arithmetic circuits over this ring, composed of addition and multiplication gates. The syntax of these algorithms is given as follows.

-Key-Generation. The algorithm **KeyGen**, on input the security parameter 1^λ, outputs (**sk**) ← **KeyGen**(1^λ) , where **sk** is a secret encryption/decryption key.

-Encryption. The algorithm **Enc**, on input system parameter $[q]$, secret keys(**sk**) and a message $m \in U$, outputs a ciphertext $C \leftarrow$**Enc**(**sk**;m).

-Decryption. The algorithm **Dec**, on input system parameter $[q]$, secret key(**sk**) and a ciphertext C, outputs a message $m^* \leftarrow$**Dec**(**sk**;C).

-Homomorphic-Evaluation. The algorithm **Eval**, on input system parameter q, an arithmetic circuit ckt, and a tuple of n ciphertexts $(C_1, \ldots, C_n)$, outputs a ciphertext $C' \leftarrow$**Eval**(ckt; $C_1, \ldots, C_n$).

The security notion needed in this scheme is security against chosen plaintext attacks (**IND-CPA** security), defined as follows.

Definition 1 (**IND-CPA security**). A scheme HE is **IND-CPA** secure if for any PPT adversary A_d it holds that:

$$\text{Adv}^{\text{CPA}}_{\text{HE}} [\lambda] := |\text{Pr}[A_d(\textbf{Enc}(\textbf{sk};0)) = 1] - \text{Pr}[A_d(\textbf{Enc}(\textbf{sk};1)) = 1]| = \text{negl}(\lambda)$$

where (**sk**) ←**KeyGen**(1^λ).

§3.2 Definition of fully homomorphic encryption

A scheme HE is fully homomorphic if it is both compact and homomorphic with respect to a

class of circuits. More formally:

Definition 2 (**Fully homomorphic encryption**). A homomorphic encryption scheme FHE :=(**KeyGen; Enc; Dec; Eval**) is fully homomorphic if it satisfies the following properties:

1. Homomorphism: Let $CR = \{CR_\lambda\}_{\lambda \in \mathbb{N}}$ be the set of all polynomial sized arithmetic circuits. On input $(\mathbf{sk}) \leftarrow \mathbf{KeyGen}(1^\lambda)$, $\forall \text{ckt} \in CR_\lambda$, $\forall (m_1,\ldots,m_n) \in M^n$ where $n = n(\lambda)$, $\forall (C_1,\ldots,C_n)$

where $C_i \leftarrow \mathbf{Enc}(\mathbf{sk};m_i)$, it holds that:

$$\Pr[\mathbf{Dec}(\mathbf{sk};\mathbf{Eval}(\text{ckt}; C_1,\ldots,C_n)) \neq \text{ckt}(m_1,\ldots,m_n)] = \text{negl}(\lambda).$$

2. Compactness: There exists a polynomial $\mu = \mu(\lambda)$ such that the output length of **Eval** is at

most μ bits long regardless of the input circuit ckt and the number of its inputs.

§3.3 Proposed fully homomorphic enciphering/deciphering functions

We propose a fully homomorphic encryption (FHE) scheme based on the enciphering/deciphering functions on octonion ring over *Fq*.
I define the some parameters for describing FHE.
Let q be a prime more than 2.
Let $M=(m_0,m_1,\ldots,m_7) \in O$ be the plaintext to be encrypted.
Let $X=(x_0,\ldots,x_7) \in O[X]$ be a variable.
Let $E(M,X)$ and $D(M,X)$ be a enciphering/deciphering function of user A.
Let $C(X)=E(M,X) \in O[X]$ be the ciphertext.
$A_i \in O$ is selected randomly such that A_i^{-1} exists $(i=1,\ldots,k)$ which is the secret keys of user A.

$C(X)=E(M,X)$ is defined as follows.

$$C(X)=E(M,X):=A_1(\ldots(A_k(M(A_k^{-1}(\ldots(A_1^{-1}X)\ldots)\bmod q \in O[X], \quad (4.34)$$

$$=(e_{00}x_0+e_{01}x_1+ \ldots +e_{07}x_7,$$

$$e_{10}x_0+e_{11}x_1+ \ldots +e_{17}x_7,$$

$$\ldots \qquad \ldots$$

$$e_{70}x_0 + e_{71}x_1 + \ldots + e_{77}x_7), \tag{4.35}$$

$$= \{e_{ij}\}(i,j=0,\ldots,7) \tag{4.36}$$

with $e_{ij} \in Fq$ $(i,j=0,\ldots,7)$ which is published in cloud centre.
Let $D(.)$ be the deciphering function defined as follows.

$$G_1(X) := A_k^{-1}(\ldots(A_1^{-1}X)\ldots), \tag{4,37}$$

$$G_2(X) := A_1(\ldots(A_kX)\ldots), \tag{4.38}$$

$D := D(C(\mathbf{1}))$

$$= G_1(C(G_2(\mathbf{1})) = A_k^{-1}(\ldots(A_1^{-1}(\ldots(A_1(\ldots(A_k(M(A_k^{-1}(\ldots(A_1^{-1}(A_1(\ldots(A_k\mathbf{1})\ldots)) \quad (4.39)$$

$$= M = (m_0, m_1, \ldots, m_7).$$

§3.4 Elements on octonion ring assumption EOR($k;q$)

Here we describe the assumption on which the proposed scheme bases on.

Elements on octonion ring assumption EOR($k;q$).

Let q be a prime more than 2. Let k be integer parameters. Let $A := (A_1, \ldots, A_k) \in O^k$, $A^{-1} := (A_1^{-1}, \ldots, A_k^{-1}) \in O^k$. Let $M_A V_{XY} := A(X,Y) = A_k(\ldots(A_1(Y(A_1^{-1}(\ldots(A_k^{-1}X)\ldots)) \bmod q \in O[X,Y]$ where $M_A := \{a_{ijk}\} \in Fq^{8 \times 64}$, $V_{XY} := (x_iy_j)^t = (x_0y_0, x_1y_0, \ldots, x_7y_7)^t \in Fq^{64 \times 1}$, X and Y are variables. In the **EOR($k;q$)** assumption, the adversary A_d is given a random matrix M_A and his goal is to find a set of elements $A = (A_1, \ldots, A_k) \in O^k$, with the order of the elements $A_1, \ldots, A_k$. For a parameter $k = k(\lambda)$ defined in terms of the security parameter λ and for any PPT adversary A_d we have

$$\Pr[A_k(\ldots(A_1(Y(A_1^{-1}(\ldots(A_k^{-1}X)\ldots)) \bmod q = M_A V_{XY}: A = (A_1, \ldots, A_k) \leftarrow A_d(1^\lambda, M_A)]$$

$$= \mathrm{negl}(\lambda).$$

To solve directly **EOR($k;q$)** assumption is known to be the problem for solving the multivariate algebraic equations of high degree which is known to be NP-hard.

§3.5 Syntax of proposed algorithms

The syntax of proposed scheme is given as follows.

-Key-Generation. The algorithm **KeyGen**, on input the security parameter 1^λ and system parameter q, outputs (**sk**)←**KeyGen**(1^λ), where **sk** is a secret encryption/dencryption key.

-Encryption. The algorithm **Enc**, on input system parameter [q], and secret keys(**sk**) and a message $m \in M$, outputs a ciphertext $C(X; \mathbf{sk}, m) \leftarrow \mathbf{Enc}(\mathbf{sk}; m)$.

-Decryption. The algorithm **Dec**, on input system parameter $[q]$, secret keys (**sk**) and a ciphertext $\{c_{ij}\}$, outputs message **Dec**(**sk**; $\{c_{ij}\}$) where $\{c_{ij}\} \leftarrow$ **Enc**(**sk**; m).

-Homomorphic-Evaluation. The algorithm **Eval**, on input system parameter q, an arithmetic circuit ckt, and a tuple of n ciphertexts $(\{c1_{ij}\}, \ldots, \{cn_{ij}\})$, outputs an evaluated ciphertext $\{c'_{ij}\} \leftarrow$ **Eval**(ckt; $\{c1_{ij}\}, \ldots, \{cn_{ij}\}$).

Theorem 4.9

For any $M, N \in O$,

$$\text{if } E(M, X) = E(N, X) \bmod q, \text{ then } M = N \bmod q.$$

That is, if $M \neq N \bmod q$, then $E(M, X) \neq E(N, X) \bmod q$.

(*Proof*)

If $E(M, X) = E(N, X) \bmod q$, then

$$A_1(\ldots(A_k(M(A_k^{-1}(\ldots(A_1^{-1}X)\ldots)) = (A_1(\ldots(A_k(N(A_k^{-1}(\ldots(A_1^{-1}X)\ldots)) \bmod q.$$

We substitute $A_1(\ldots(A_kX)\ldots)$ to X in above expression, we obtain

$$A_1(\ldots(A_k(M(A_k^{-1}(\ldots(A_1^{-1}(A_1(\ldots(A_kX)\ldots)$$

$$= A_1(\ldots(A_k(N(A_k^{-1}(\ldots(A_1^{-1}(A_1(\ldots(A_kX)\ldots)) \bmod q$$

$$A_1(\ldots(A_k(MX)\ldots) = A_1(\ldots(A_k(NX)\ldots) \bmod q$$

$$MX = NX \bmod q$$

We substitute **1** to X,

$$M = N \bmod q. \qquad\qquad \text{q.e.d}$$

It is said that M and $E(M, X)$ corresponds one to one.

It is shown that the encrypting function $E(M, X)$ has the property of fully homomorphism.

§3.6 Addition/subtraction scheme on ciphertexts

Let $N = (n_0, n_1, \ldots, n_7) \in O$ be another plaintext to be encrypted.

Let $C_1(X) = E(M, X)$ and $C_2(X) = E(N, X)$ be the ciphertexts.

$C_1(X) \pm C_2(X) \bmod q = E(M,X) \pm E(N,X) \bmod q$

$= A_1(\ldots(A_k(M(A_k^{-1}(\ldots(A_1^{-1}X)\ldots) + A_1(\ldots(A_k(N(A_k^{-1}(\ldots(A_1^{-1}X)\ldots)) \bmod q$

$= A_1(\ldots(A_k([M \pm N](A_k^{-1}(\ldots(A_1^{-1}X)\ldots)) \bmod q$

$E(M,X) \pm E(N,X) = E(M \pm N, X) \bmod q. \hfill (4.40)$

§3.7 Multiplication scheme on ciphertexts

Let $C_1(X) = E(M, X)$ and $C_2(X) = E(N, X)$ be the ciphertexts.

$C_1(C_2(X)) \bmod q = E(M, E(N,X)) \bmod q$

$= A_1(\ldots(A_k(M(A_k^{-1}(A_1^{-1}(A_1(\ldots(A_k(N(A_k^{-1}(\ldots(A_1^{-1}X)\ldots)) \bmod q$

$= A_1(\ldots(A_k(M(N(A_k^{-1}(\ldots(A_1^{-1}X)\ldots)) \bmod q \hfill (4.41)$

§3.8 Inverse of $E(M,X)$

We define $E(M, X)^{(-1)}$, the inverse of $E(M, X)$ such that

$$E(M, E(M, X)^{(-1)}) = E(M, E(M, X))^{(-1)} = X. \hfill (4.42)$$

Theorem 4.10

In case that $M \in O$ has the inverse, that is $|M|^2 \neq 0 \bmod q$,
if $E(M, E(M', X)) = E(M', E(M, X)) = X$,

$$M' = M^{-1} \bmod q,$$

That is,

$$E(M, X)^{(-1)} = E(M^{-1}, X).$$

(*Proof:*)

$E(M, E(M',X))$

$= A_1(\ldots(A_k(M(A_k^{-1}(\ldots(A_1^{-1}(A_1(\ldots(A_k(M'(A_k^{-1}(\ldots(A_1^{-1}X)\ldots)) \bmod q = X$

$A_1(\ldots(A_k(M(M'(A_k^{-1}(\ldots(A_1^{-1}X)\ldots)) \bmod q = X$

We substitute $(A_1(\ldots(A_k \mathbf{1})\ldots)$ to X in above expression, we obtain

$$A_1(\ldots(A_k(MM'))\ldots) = (A_1(\ldots(A_k\mathbf{1})\ldots) \bmod q.$$

$$MM' = \mathbf{1} \bmod q,$$

Then

$$M'=M^{-1} \bmod q,$$

That is

$$E(M, X)^{(-1)}=E(M^{-1}, X).$$

As the same manner, we obtain the same result from the equation

$$E(M', E(M, X))=X. \qquad \text{q.e.d.}$$

We define the element expression of $E(M, X)$ and $E(M', X)$ which is the inverse of $E(M, X)$ as follows.

$$E(M, X)=A_1(...(A_k(M(A_k^{-1}(...(A_1^{-1}X)...) \bmod q \in O[X],$$

$$=(\, e_{00}x_0+e_{01}x_1+ ... +e_{07}x_7,$$

$$e_{10}x_0+e_{11}x_1+ ... +e_{17}x_7,$$

....

$$e_{70}x_0+e_{71}x_1+ ... +e_{77}x_7) \bmod q, \tag{4..43}$$

$$=\{e_{ij}\}(i,j=0,...,7) \tag{4.44}$$

with $e_{ij} \in \boldsymbol{Fq}\ (i,j=0,...,7)$.

$$E(M', X)=A_1(...(A_k(M'(A_k^{-1}(...(A_1^{-1}X)...) \bmod q \in O[X],$$

$$=(\, e'_{00}x_0+e'_{01}x_1+ ... +e'_{07}x_7,$$

$$e'_{10}x_0+e'_{11}x_1+ ... +e'_{17}x_7,$$

....

$$e'_{70}x_0+e'_{71}x_1+ ... +e'_{77}x_7) \bmod q, \tag{4.45}$$

$$=\{e'_{ij}\}(i,j=0,...,7) \tag{4.46}$$

with $e'_{ij} \in \boldsymbol{Fq}\ (i,j=0,...,7)$.

Then we obtain

$$E(M, E(M', X)) =$$

$\{e_{00}(e'_{00}x_0+e'_{01}x_1+...+e'_{07}x_7)+e_{01}(e'_{10}x_0+e'_{11}x_1+...+e'_{17}x_7)+... +e_{07}(e'_{70}x_0+e'_{71}x_1+...+e'_{77}x_7),$

$e_{10}(e'_{00}x_0 + e'_{01}x_1 + \ldots + e'_{07}x_7) + e_{11}(e'_{10}x_0 + e'_{11}x_1 + \ldots + e'_{17}x_7) + \ldots + e_{17}(e'_{70}x_0 + e'_{71}x_1 + \ldots + e'_{77}x_7),$

....

$e_{70}(e'_{00}x_0 + e'_{01}x_1 + \ldots + e'_{07}x_7) + e_{71}(e'_{10}x_0 + e'_{11}x_1 + \ldots + e'_{17}x_7) + \ldots + e_{77}(e'_{70}x_0 + e'_{71}x_1 + \ldots + e'_{77}x_7)\}$

mod q.

From

$$E(M, E(M', X)) = X = (x_0, \ldots, x_7) \bmod q,$$

We obtain

$$e_{00}e'_{00} + e_{01}e'_{10} + \ldots + e_{07}e'_{70} = 1 \bmod q$$
$$e_{10}e'_{00} + e_{11}e'_{10} + \ldots + e_{17}e'_{70} = 0 \bmod q$$
$$\bullet \ \bullet \ \bullet \quad \bullet \ \bullet \ \bullet$$
$$e_{70}e'_{00} + e_{71}e'_{10} + \ldots + e_{77}e'_{70} = 0 \bmod q$$

$$e_{00}e'_{01} + e_{01}e'_{11} + \ldots + e_{07}e'_{71} = 0 \bmod q$$
$$e_{10}e'_{01} + e_{11}e'_{11} + \ldots + e_{17}e'_{71} = 1 \bmod q$$
$$\bullet \ \bullet \ \bullet \quad \bullet \ \bullet \ \bullet$$
$$e_{70}e'_{01} + e_{71}e'_{11} + \ldots + e_{77}e'_{71} = 0 \bmod q$$

$$\bullet \ \bullet \ \bullet \quad \bullet \ \bullet \ \bullet$$

$$\bullet \ \bullet \ \bullet \quad \bullet \ \bullet \ \bullet$$

$$e_{00}e'_{07} + e_{01}e'_{17} + \ldots + e_{07}e'_{77} = 0 \bmod q$$
$$e_{10}e'_{07} + e_{11}e'_{17} + \ldots + e_{17}e'_{77} = 0 \bmod q$$
$$\bullet \ \bullet \ \bullet \quad \bullet \ \bullet \ \bullet$$
$$e_{70}e'_{07} + e_{71}e'_{17} + \ldots + e_{77}e'_{77} = 1 \bmod q$$

We solve the above 8 simultaneous equations so that we obtain the value of $e'_y \in$

$Fq(i,j=0,\ldots,7).$

That is,

$$E(M, X)^{(-1)}=E(M^{-1}, X) \bmod q$$

$$=(e'_{00}x_0+e'_{01}x_1+ \ldots +e'_{07}x_7,$$

$$e'_{10}x_0+e'_{11}x_1+ \ldots +e'_{17} x_7,$$

....

$$e'_{70}x_0+e'_{71}x_1+ \ldots +e'_{77} x_7) \bmod q, \tag{4.47}$$

$$=\{e'_{ij}\}(i,j=0,\ldots,7) \tag{4.48}$$

with $e'_{ij} \in Fq$ $(i,j=0,\ldots,7).$

§3.9 Division scheme on ciphertexts

Let $C_1(X)= E(M, X)$ and $C_2(X)= E (N, X)$ be the ciphertexts.

We try to make the ciphertext of M/N where N has the inverse.

First we calculate the inverse of $E(N,X)$ by using method described above to obtain $E(N,X)^{(-1)},$

$$E(N, X)^{(-1)}= E (N^{-1}, X).$$

$$E(M, E(N, X)^{(-1)})= E(M, E(N^{-1}, X))$$

$$=A_1(\ldots(A_k(M(N^{-1}(A_k^{-1} (\ldots(A_1^{-1}X)\ldots) \bmod q \in O[X] \tag{4.49}$$

§3.10 Property of proposed fully homomorphic encryption

(IND-CPA security). Proposed fully homomorphic encryption is IND-CPA secure.

As adversary A_d does not know sk, A_d is not able to calculate M from the value of $E(M,X).$

For any PPT adversary A_d it holds that:

$$\mathrm{Adv^{CPA}_{HE}} [\lambda] :=|\Pr[A_d(E(M_0,X)) = 1] - \Pr[A_d((E(M_1,X))= 1]|= \mathrm{negl}(\lambda)$$

where (sk) ←KeyGen(1^λ).

(Fully homomorphic encryption). Proposed fully homomorphic encryption =(KeyGen; Enc; Dec; Eval) is fully homomorphic because it satisfies the following properties:

1. Homomorphism: Let $CR = \{CR_\lambda\}_{\lambda \in N}$ be the set of all polynomial sized arithmetic circuits. On input $(\mathbf{sk}) \leftarrow \mathbf{KeyGen}(1^k)$, $\forall \mathrm{ckt} \in CR_\lambda$, $\forall (m_1,\ldots,m_n) \in M^n$ where n $= n(\lambda)$, $\forall(\{c_{1ij}\},\ldots,\{c_{nij}\})$ where $\{c_{rij}\} \leftarrow (E(M_r,X))$, $(r=1,\ldots,n)$, we have $D(\mathbf{sk};\mathbf{Eval}(\mathrm{ckt}; \{c_{1ij}\},\ldots,\{c_{nij}\})) = \mathrm{ckt}(m_1,\ldots,m_n)$.

Then it holds that:

$$\Pr[D(\mathbf{sk}; \mathbf{Eval}(\mathrm{ckt}; \{c_{1ij}\},\ldots,\{c_{nij}\})) \neq \mathrm{ckt}(m_1,\ldots,m_n)] = \mathrm{negl}(\lambda).$$

2. Compactness: As the output length of **Eval** is at most $k\log_2 q = k\lambda$ where k is a positive integer, there exists a polynomial $\mu = \mu(\lambda)$ such that the output length of **Eval** is at most μ bits long regardless of the input circuit ckt and the number of its inputs.

§4. Proposed fully homomorphic data-processing procedure

User A is the data holder generating the ciphertexts corresponding to the data which he holds. He wants that the information of the data which he holds is not revealed.

User B is the company which processes the enciphered data in cloud data centre without revealing and knowing the information of the data.

User A wants to obtain the result for processing the data, for example, stochastic value.

1) User A selects $A_i \in O$ randomly such that A_i^{-1} exists $(i=1,\ldots,k)$ which is the secret keys of user A.

Let $M_i(i=0,\ldots,n-1)$ be the plaintexts.

$C(X)=E(M_i, X)$ is defined as follows.

$$C(X)=E(M_i, X)=A_1(\ldots(A_k(M_i(A_k^{-1}(\ldots(A_1^{-1}X)\ldots)\ldots) \bmod q \in O[X], \quad (4.50a)$$

$$=(ei_{00}x_0 + ei_{01}x_1 + \ldots + ei_{07}x_7,$$

$$ei_{10}x_0 + ei_{11}x_1 + \ldots + ei_{17}x_7,$$

$$\ldots \qquad \ldots$$

$$ei_{70}x_0 + ei_{71}x_1 + \ldots + ei_{77}x_7), \qquad\qquad\qquad (4.50b)$$

$$= \{ei_{jk}\}(j,k=0,\ldots,7) \qquad\qquad\qquad (4.50c)$$

with $ei_{jk} \in Fq$ $(i=0,\ldots,n-1; j,k=0,\ldots,7)$.

2) User A encrypts plaintexts $M_i \in O$ $(i=0,\ldots,n-1)$ to $C_i(X) \in O[X]$ $(i=0,\ldots,n-1)$ such that

$$C_i(X)=E(M_i, X) \ (i=0,1,\ldots,n-1)$$

where $E(.)$ is the enciphering function to be secret.

3) User A sends $[ei_{jk}\ (i=0,\ldots,n\text{-}1;j,k=0,\ldots,7)]$ to cloud data centre through the insecure line.

4) Later, user A sends his request for processing the data of user A to the user B.

For example 1, user A requests the value of the ciphertext corresponding to $(M_1+M_2+M_3)/(M_2M_3)\in O.$

5) User B receives the request from user A and downloads $q,C_1(X),C_2(X),C_3(X)$ from cloud data centre.He calculates the ciphertext $C^*(X)$ corresponding to $(M_1+M_2+M_3)/(M_2M_3)$ as follows.

$$C_1(X)=E(M_1,X)=A_1(\ldots(A_k(M_1\ (A_k^{-1}\ (\ldots(A_1^{-1}X)\ldots)\ \text{mod}\ q, \tag{4.51}$$

$$C_2(X)=E(M_2,X)=A_1(\ldots(A_k(M_2(A_k^{-1}\ (\ldots(A_1^{-1}X)\ldots)\ \text{mod}\ q, \tag{4.52}$$

$$C_3(X)=E(M_3,X)=A_1(\ldots(A_k(M_3(A_k^{-1}\ (\ldots(A_1^{-1}X)\ldots)\ \text{mod}\ q, \tag{4.53}$$

$$K_1(X)=C_1(X)+C_2(X)+C_3(X)=A_1(\ldots(A_k([M_1+M_2+M_3](A_k^{-1}(\ldots(A_1^{-1}X)\ldots)\ \text{mod}\ q,\tag{4.54}$$

$$K_2(X)=C_2(C_3(X))=E(M_2,E(M_3,X))=A_1(\ldots(A_k(M_2(M_3(A_k^{-1}(\ldots(A_1^{-1}X)\ldots)\ \text{mod}\ q,\tag{4.55}$$

$$K_3(X)=K_2(X)^{(-1)}\ \text{mod}\ q, \tag{4.56}$$

where $K_3(K_2(X)) = K_2(K_3(X)\ )=X\ \text{mod}\ q.$

$K_3(X)$ is obtained by using the method described in §3.8 Inverse of $E(M,X)$ and applying to

$K_2(X)^{(-1)}.$

Then $K_3(X)$ is given such that

$$K_3(X)=A_1(\ldots(A_k(M_3^{-1}\ (M_2^{-1}\ (A_k^{-1}\ (\ldots(A_1^{-1}X)\ldots)\ \text{mod}\ q, \tag{4.57}$$

because

$$A_1(\ldots(A_k(M_2(M_3\ (A_k^{-1}\ (\ldots(A_1^{-1}\ (A_1(\ldots(A_k(M_3^{-1}\ (M_2^{-1}\ (A_k^{-1}\ (\ldots(A_1^{-1}X)\ldots)$$

$$= A_1(\ldots(A_k(M_2(M_3\ (M_3^{-1}\ (M_2^{-1}\ (A_k^{-1}\ (\ldots(A_1^{-1}X)\ldots)$$

$$= A_1(\ldots(A_k(M_2(M_3\ (M_3^{-1}\ (M_2^{-1}\ (A_k^{-1}\ (\ldots(A_1^{-1}X)\ldots)=X\ \text{mod}\ q. \tag{4.58}$$

$$C^*(X)=K_1(K_3(X))\ \text{mod}\ q. \tag{4.59a}$$

$$=(c_{00}x_0+\ldots c_{07}x_7,$$

$$\ldots\qquad\ldots$$

$$c_{70}x_0+\ldots+c_{77}x_7) \tag{4.59b}$$

$$=\{c_{ij}\}(i,j=0,\ldots,7) \tag{4.59c}$$

with $c_{ij} \in Fq$ $(i,j=0,\ldots,7)$.

6) User B sends $C^*(X)$ as the ciphertext corresponding to the plaintext $(M_1+M_2+M_3)/(M_2M_3)$ to user A.

7) User A receives $C^*(X)$ from user B.

8) User A deciphers $C^*(X)$ to obtain the plaintext $(M_1+M_2+M_3)/(M_2M_3)$ by using the secret keys of user A, $A_i(i=0,\ldots,k)$ such that

$$A_k^{-1}(\ldots(A_1^{-1}(C^*[A_1(\ldots(A_k1)\ldots)]\ldots)$$

$$= A_k^{-1}(\ldots(A_1^{-1}\{K_1(K_3[A_1(\ldots(A_k1)\ldots)])\})\ldots)$$

$$=A_k^{-1}(\ldots(A_1^{-1}(A_1(\ldots(A_k\{[M_1+M_2+M_3](A_k^{-1}(\ldots(A_1^{-1}(A_1(\ldots(A_k(M_3^{-1}(M_2^{-1}(A_k^{-1}(\ldots(A_1^{-1}$$

$$(A_1(\ldots(A_k1)\ldots)\}\ldots)$$

$$=[M_1+M_2+M_3](M_3^{-1}(M_2^{-1}(A_k^{-1}(\ldots(A_1^{-1}(A_1(\ldots(A_k1)\ldots)$$

$$=[M_1+M_2+M_3](M_3^{-1}(M_2^{-1}))$$

$$=[M_1+M_2+M_3](M_2M_3)^{-1}$$

$$=[M_1+M_2+M_3]/(M_2M_3) \bmod q. \tag{4.60}$$

(See Fig.4.1)

9) Next user A sends his request for processing the data of user A to the user B. For example No.2, user A requests the value of the ciphertext corresponding to $(M_1+M_2+M_3)/(M_1+M_2M_3) \in O$.

10) User B receives the request from user A and he calculates the ciphertext $C^*(X)$ corresponding to $(M_1+M_2+M_3)/(M_1+M_2M_3)$ as follows.

$$C_1(X)=E(M_1,X)=A_1(\ldots(A_k(M_1(A_k^{-1}(\ldots(A_1^{-1}X)\ldots) \bmod q, \tag{4.61}$$

$$C_2(X)=E(M_2,X)=A_1(\ldots(A_k(M_2(A_k^{-1}(\ldots(A_1^{-1}X)\ldots) \bmod q, \tag{4.62}$$

$$C_3(X)=E(M_3,X)=A_1(\ldots(A_k(M_3(A_k^{-1}(\ldots(A_1^{-1}X)\ldots) \bmod q, \tag{4.63}$$

$$K_1(X)=C_1(X)+C_2(X)+C_3(X)=A_1(\ldots(A_k([M_1+M_2+M_3](A_k^{-1}(\ldots(A_1^{-1}X)\ldots) \bmod q, \tag{4.64}$$

$$K_2(X)=C_2(C_3(X))=E(M_2,E(M_3,X))=A_1(\ldots(A_k(M_2(M_3(A_k^{-1}(\ldots(A_1^{-1}X)\ldots) \bmod q, \tag{4.65}$$

$$K_3(X)= C_1(X)+K_2(X)$$

$$=A_1(\ldots(A_k(M_1(A_k^{-1}(\ldots(A_1^{-1}X)\ldots)+A_1(\ldots(A_k(M_2(M_3(A_k^{-1}(\ldots(A_1^{-1}X)\ldots) \bmod q,$$

$$=A_1(\ldots(A_k[M_1(A_k^{-1}(\ldots(A_1^{-1}X)\ldots)+M_2(M_3(A_k^{-1}(\ldots(A_1^{-1}X)\ldots)])\ldots) \bmod q, \tag{4.66}$$

Let

$C_1*(X) := K_1(X)$ (4.67)

and

$C_2*(X) := K_3(X).$ (4.68)

11) User B sends $C_1*(X) = K_1(X)$ and $C_2*(X) = K_3(X)$ as the ciphertext to user A.

12) User A receives $C_1*(X) = K_1(X)$ and $C_2*(X) = K_3(X)$ from user B.

13) User A deciphers $C_1*(X) = K_1(X)$ and $C_2*(X) = K_3(X)$ to obtain the plaintext $(M_1 + M_2 + M_3)/$

  $(M_1 + M_2 M_3)$ by using the secret keys of user A as follows.

$R_1 := A_k^{-1}(\ldots(A_1^{-1}(C_1*(A_1(\ldots(A_k 1)\ldots))$

$= A_k^{-1}(\ldots(A_1^{-1}(K_1(A_1(\ldots(A_k 1)\ldots)\ldots)$

$= M_1 + M_2 + M_3 \bmod q,$ (4.69)

$R_2 := A_k^{-1}(\ldots(A_1^{-1}(C_2*(A_1(\ldots(A_k 1)\ldots))$

$= A_k^{-1}(\ldots(A_1^{-1}(A_1(\ldots(A_k[M_1(A_k^{-1}(\ldots(A_1^{-1}(A_1(\ldots(A_k 1)\ldots))$

$\qquad\qquad + M_2(M_3(A_k^{-1}(\ldots(A_1^{-1}(A_1(\ldots(A_k 1)\ldots))])\ldots),$

$= M_1 + M_2(M_3\ 1) \bmod q,$

$= M_1 + M_2 M_3 \bmod q.$ (4.70)

$R_1(R_2)^{-1} = (M_1 + M_2 + M_3)(M_1 + M_2 M_3)^{-1} \bmod q$

$= (M_1 + M_2 + M_3)/(M_1 + M_2 M_3) \bmod q.$ (4.71)

Here we notice that from theorem 4.11, $D \in O$ does not exist such that
$C_2*(X) = A_k^{-1}(\ldots(A_1^{-1}(A_1(\ldots(A_k(D(A_k^{-1}(\ldots(A_1^{-1}(A_1(\ldots(A_k 1)\ldots).$

Theorem 4.11
Let $M_1, M_2, M_3 \in O$ be non-associative each other.
$D \in O$ does not exist such that

$$M_1 X + M_2(M_3 X) = DX.$$

(*Proof.*)
When $X = 1$, we obtain

$$M_1 + M_2 M_3 = D.$$

Then

$$M_1X+M_2(M_3X)=(M_1+M_2M_3)X \qquad \text{①}$$

Let E be non-associative to M_2,M_3, that is,

$$M_2(M_3E)\neq(M_2M_3)E. \qquad \text{②}$$

From ①, when $X=E$,

$$M_1E+M_2(M_3E)=(M_1+M_2M_3)E$$

$$M_2(M_3E)=(M_2M_3)E \qquad \text{③}$$

It is contradictory.

q.e.d.

§5. Proposed re-encryption scheme

Now I describe the re-encryption schemes on octonion ring over Fq by using the proposed enciphering/deciphering functions. (See Fig.4.2)

User A selects $A_i \in O$ randomly such that A_i^{-1} exists ($i=1,...,k$) which is the secret keys of user A.

User A selects $B_i \in O$ randomly such that B_i^{-1} exists ($i=1,...,k$) which is the secret keys of user A.

Let M_i be a plaintext ($i=0,...,n-1$).

Ciphertext $E(M_i,X;A)$ *is* defined as follows.

$$E(M_i,X;A)=A_1(...(A_k(M_i(A_k^{-1}(...(A_1^{-1}X)...)\bmod q \in O[X], \qquad (4.72a)$$

$$= (ei_{00}x_0+ei_{01}x_1+ ...+ei_{07}x_7,$$

$$ei_{10}x_0+ei_{11}x_1+ ...+ei_{17}x_7,$$

$$....\qquad\qquad....$$

$$ei_{70}x_0+ei_{71}x_1+ ...+ei_{77}x_7)\quad \bmod q, \qquad (4.72b)$$

$$=\{ei_{jk}\}(\ i=0,...,n-1;j,k=0,...,7) \qquad (4.72c)$$

with $ei_{jk}\in Fq$ ($i=0,...,n-1;j,k=0,...,7$) which is the secret keys of user A.

We show how to re-encipher $E(M_i,X;A)$ *to* $E(M_i,X;B)$ by using $B_i \in O$ as follows.

$$C_{A-B}=B_1(...(B_k(A_k^{-1}(...(A_1^{-1}(E[M_i,A_1(...(A_k(B_k^{-1}(...(B_1^{-1}X)...);A])...)\bmod q \quad (4.73a)$$

$$= B_1(...(B_k(M_i(B_k^{-1}(...(B_1^{-1}X)...)\bmod q$$

$$= E(M_i,X;B) \qquad (4.73b)$$

User A sends the re-encryption keys $K_{RE}1$, $K_{RE}2$ to cloud data centre.

$$K_{RE}1(X):= B_1(\dots(B_k(A_k^{-1}(\dots(A_1^{-1}(X))\dots) \text{ mod } q, \qquad (4.74)$$

$$K_{RE}2(X):= A_1(\dots(A_k(B_k^{-1}(\dots(B_1^{-1}X))\dots) \text{ mod } q, \qquad (4.75)$$

where we notice that

$$K_{RE}1(K_{RE}2(X))$$

$$= B_1(\dots(B_k(A_k^{-1}(\dots(A_1^{-1}(A_1(\dots(A_k(B_k^{-1}(\dots(B_1^{-1}X))\dots))\dots)=X \quad \text{mod } q. \qquad (4.76)$$

Cloud data centre replaces $E(M_i,X;A)$ into $E(M_i,X;B)$ by using the re-encryption keys $K_{RE}1(X)$, $K_{RE}2(X)$ as follows.

$$K_{RE}1(E(M_i, K_{RE}2(X);A))= E(M_i, X;B)\ (i=0,\dots,n\text{-}1). \qquad (4.77)$$

Cloud data centre sends $E(M_i,X;B)$ to user B who wants information $M_i(i=0,\dots,n\text{-}1)$. User A sends the $K_{DE}1(X)$, $K_{DE}2(X)$ to user B such that

$$K_{DE}1(X):= B_1(\dots(B_k(X)\dots) \quad \text{mod } q, \qquad (4.78)$$

$$K_{DE}2(X):= B_k^{-1}(\dots(B_1^{-1}X)\dots) \text{ mod } q, \qquad (4.79)$$

where we notice that

$$K_{DE}1(K_{DE}2(X))=X \text{ mod } q. \qquad (4.80)$$

User B deciphers $E(M_i,X;B)$ to obtain M_i as follows.

$$K_{DE}2(\ E(M_i, K_{DE}1(X);B))=M_i \quad \text{mod } q\ (i=0,\dots,n\text{-}1). \qquad (4.81)$$

§6. Analysis of proposed scheme

Here we analyze the proposed fully homomorphism encryption scheme.

§6.1 Computing plaintext M and A_i ($i=1,\dots,k$) from coefficients of ciphertext $E(M,X;A)$ to be published

Ciphertext $E(M,X;A)$ is published by cloud data centre as follows.

$$E(M,X;A)=A_1(\dots(A_k(M(A_k^{-1}(\dots(A_1^{-1}X)\dots) \text{ mod } q \in O[X]\ , \qquad (4.82a)$$

$$=(\ e_{00}x_0+e_{01}x_1+\ \dots+e_{07}x_7,$$

$$e_{10}x_0+e_{11}x_1+\ \dots+e_{17}\ x_7,$$

....

$$e_{70}x_0+e_{71}x_1+ ... +e_{77}x_7) \quad \text{mod } q, \tag{4.82b}$$

$$=\{e_{jr}\}(j,r=0,...,7) \tag{4.82c}$$

with $e_{jr} \in Fq$ ($j,r=0,...,7$) which is published,
where $A_i \in O$ to be selected randomly such that A_i^{-1} exists ($i=1,...,k$) are the secret keys of user A.

We try to find plaintext M from coefficients of $E(M,X;A)$, $e_{jr} \in Fq$ ($j,r=0,...,7$).

In case that $n=7$, the number of unknown variables (M, A_i ($i=1,...,7$)) is 64, the number of equations is 65 such that

$$|E(M,1;A)|^2=e_{00}^2+e_{10}^2+...+e_{70}^2 =|M|^2= m_0^2+m_1^2+...+m_7^2 \text{ mod } q, \tag{4.83}$$

$$F_{00}(M,A_1,A_2,...,A_7)=e_{00} \text{ mod } q,$$

$$F_{01}(M,A_1,A_2,...,A_7)=e_{01} \text{ mod } q,$$

$$\cdot \cdot \cdot \qquad \cdot \cdot \cdot$$

$$F_{07}(M,A_1,A_2,...,A_7)=e_{07} \text{ mod } q, \tag{4.84}$$

$$\cdot \cdot \cdot \qquad \cdot \cdot \cdot$$

$$\cdot \cdot \cdot \qquad \cdot \cdot \cdot$$

$$F_{77}(M,A_1,A_2,...,A_7)=e_{77} \text{ mod } q,$$

where $F_{00},...,F_{77}$ are the 15th algebraic multivariate equations.

Then the complexity G required for solving above simultaneous equations by using Gröbner basis is given [1.1] such as

$$G=(_{64+dreg}C_{dreg})^w =(_{512}C_{64})^w=O(2^{655}) >> O(2^{80}), \tag{4.85}$$

where w=2.39, and

$$d_{reg} = 448(=64*(15-1)/2+(2-1)/2 - 0\sqrt{} \ (64*(225-1)/6+(4-1)/6)). \tag{4.86}$$

Next we try to find plaintexts M_1 and M_2 from two ciphertexts such as

$$E(M_1,X;A)=A_1(...(A_k(M_1(A_k^{-1} (...(A_1^{-1}X)...) \text{ mod } q \in O[X] , \tag{4.87}$$

$$E(M_2,X;A)=A_1(...(A_k(M_2(A_k^{-1} (...(A_1^{-1}X)...) \text{ mod } q \in O[X]. \tag{4.88}$$

We obtain 130 equations as follows.

$$|E(M_i,1;A)|^2 = e_{i00}^2 + e_{i10}^2 + \ldots + e_{i70}^2 = |M_i|^2 = m_{i0}^2 + m_{i1}^2 + \ldots + m_{i7}^2 \bmod q, \tag{4.89}$$

$$F_{00}(M_i,A_1,A_2,\ldots,A_7) = e_{i00} \bmod q,$$

$$F_{01}(M_i,A_1,A_2,\ldots,A_7) = e_{i01} \bmod q,$$

$$\cdots \qquad \cdots$$

$$F_{07}(M_i,A_1,A_2,\ldots,A_7) = e_{i07} \bmod q, \tag{4.90}$$

$$\cdots \qquad \cdots$$

$$\cdots \qquad \cdots$$

$$F_{77}(M_i,A_1,A_2,\ldots,A_7) = e_{i77} \bmod q,$$

$$(i=1,2),$$

where $F_{00},\ldots, F_{77}$ are the 15th algebraic multivariate equations.

The number of unknown variables $(M_1, M_2, A_i\,(i=1,\ldots,7))$ is 72, and the number of equations is 130.

Then the complexity G required for solving above simultaneous equations by using Gröbner basis is given such that

$$G = ({}_{72+dreg}C_{dreg})^w, \tag{4.91}$$

where we are not able to compute the d_{reg} accurately.

So we adopt 15 as d_{reg}.

$$G > G' = ({}_{72+dreg}C_{dreg})^w = ({}_{87}C_{15})^w = O(2^{130}) \gg O(2^{80}). \tag{4.92}$$

The complexity G required for solving above simultaneous equations by using Gröbner basis is enough large for secure.

§6.2 Computing plaintext M_i and d_{ijk} $(i,j,k=0,\ldots,7)$

We try to computing plaintext M_i and d_{ijk} $(i,j,k=0,\ldots,7)$ from coefficients of ciphertext $E(M_i,X;A)$ to be published.

At first let $E(Y,X,A) \in O[X,Y]$ be the enciphering function such as

$$E(Y,X;A) := A_1(\ldots(A_k(Y(A_k^{-1}(\ldots(A_1{}^{-1}X)\ldots)\bmod q \in O[X,Y], \tag{4.93a}$$

$$= (d_{000}x_0y_0 + d_{001}x_0y_1 + \ldots + d_{077}x_7y_7,$$

$$d_{100}x_0y_0 + d_{101}x_0y_1 + \ldots + d_{177}x_7y_7,$$

$$\cdots \qquad \cdots$$

$$d_{700}x_0y_0 + d_{701}x_0y_1 + \ldots + d_{777}x_7y_7) \bmod q, \tag{4.93b}$$

$$= \{d_{ijk}\}(i,j,k=0,\ldots,7) \tag{4.93c}$$

with $d_{ijk} \in Fq \; (i,j,k=0,\ldots,7)$.

Next we substitute M_i to Y, where

$$M_i = (m_{i0}, m_{i1}, \ldots, m_{i7}) \in O. \tag{4.94}$$
$$E(M_i, X; A) := A_1(\ldots(A_k(M_i (A_k^{-1} (\ldots(A_1^{-1}X)\ldots) \bmod q \in \quad O[X], \tag{4.95a}$$
$$= (d_{000}x_0m_0 + d_{001}x_0m_1 + \ldots + d_{077}x_7m_7,$$

$$d_{100}x_0m_0 + d_{101}x_0m_1 + \ldots + d_{177}x_7m_7,$$

$$\ldots \qquad \ldots$$

$$d_{700}x_0m_0 + d_{701}x_0m_1 + \ldots + d_{777}x_7m_7) \bmod q, \tag{4.95b}$$

$$= \{d_{ijk}\}(i,j,k=0,\ldots,7) \tag{4.95c}$$

with $d_{ijk} \in Fq \; (i,j,k=0,\ldots,7)$.

Then we obtain 64 equations from (4.43) and (4.95b) as follows.

$$
\left.
\begin{aligned}
d_{000}m_0 + d_{001}m_1 + \ldots + d_{007}m_7 &= e_{00}\\
d_{010}m_0 + d_{011}m_1 + \ldots + d_{017}m_7 &= e_{01}\\
\ldots \qquad \ldots \qquad\\
d_{070}m_0 + d_{071}m_1 + \ldots + d_{077}m_7 &= e_{07}
\end{aligned}
\right\} \tag{4.96a}
$$

$$
\left.
\begin{aligned}
d_{100}m_0 + d_{101}m_1 + \ldots + d_{107}m_7 &= e_{10}\\
d_{110}m_0 + d_{111}m_1 + \ldots + d_{117}m_7 &= e_{11}\\
\ldots \qquad \ldots \qquad\\
d_{170}m_0 + d_{171}m_1 + \ldots + d_{177}m_7 &= e_{17}
\end{aligned}
\right\} \tag{4.96b}
$$

$$\ldots \qquad \ldots$$
$$\ldots \qquad \ldots$$

$$
\left.
\begin{aligned}
d_{700}m_0 + d_{701}m_1 + \ldots + d_{707}m_7 &= e_{70}\\
d_{710}m_0 + d_{711}m_1 + \ldots + d_{717}m_7 &= e_{71}\\
\ldots \qquad \ldots \qquad
\end{aligned}
\right\} \tag{4.96c}
$$

$$d_{770}m_0+d_{771}m_1+ \ldots +d_{777}m_7=e_{77}$$

For $M_1,\ldots, M_8$ we obtain the same equations, the number of which is 512. We also obtain the 8 equations such as

$$|E(M_i,\mathbf{1};A)|^2= |M_i|^2= m_{i0}{}^2+m_{i1}{}^2+\ldots+m_{i7}{}^2 \bmod q,(i=0,\ldots,7). \qquad (4.97)$$

The number of unknown variables M_i and e_{ijk} $(i,j,k=0,\ldots,7)$ is $576(=512+64)$. The number of equations is $520(=512+8)$.

Then the complexity G required for solving above simultaneous quadratic algebraic equations by using Gröbner basis is given such as

$$G{\approx}G'=({}_{520+dreg}C_{dreg})^w =({}_{763}C_{243})^w=O(2^{1634})\gg 2^{80}, \qquad (4.98)$$

where G' is the complexity required for solving 520 simultaneous quadratic algebraic equations with 520 variables by using Gröbner basis,

where $w=2.39$,

and

$$d_{reg} = 243(=520*(2-1)/2 - \sqrt{(520*(4-1)/6)} \qquad (4.99)$$

It is thought to be difficult computationally to solve the above simultaneous algebraic equations by using Gröbner basis.

§7. The size of the modulus q and the complexity for enciphering/

deciphering

We consider the size of the system parameter q. We select the size of q such that $O(q^8)$, the order of the plaintext is larger than $O(2^{80})$. Then we need to select modulus q $=O(2^{10})$.

In case of $k=7$, $q=O(2^{10})$, the size of $e_{ij}\in Fq$ $(i,j=0,\ldots,7)$ which are the coefficients of elements in $E(M,X;A)=A_1(\ldots(A_k(M(A_k^{-1} (\ldots(A_1{}^{-1}X)\ldots)) \bmod q \in O[X]$ is $(64)(\log_2 q)$bits $=640$bits, and the size of system parameters $[q]$ is less than 20bits.

In case of $k=7$, $q=O(2^{10})$, the complexity to obtain $E(M,X;A)$ is

$$(15*512+14*36)(\log_2 q)^2= O(2^{20}) \text{ bit-operations}$$

and the complexity required for deciphering is

$$(576)(\log_2 q)^2 = O(2^{16}) \text{ bit-operations.}$$

The complexity to obtain $E(M,X;A)$ by using the element expression of $E(M,X;A)$ is

$$(512)(\log_2 q)^2 = O(2^{16}) \text{ bit-operations.}$$

On the other hand the complexity of the enciphering and deciphering in RSA scheme is

$$O(2(\log n)^3) = O(2^{34}) \text{ bit-operations}$$

where the size of modulus n is 2048bits.

Then our scheme requires small memory space and complexity to encipher and decipher so that we are able to implement our scheme to the mobile device.

§8. Conclusion of chapter 4

We proposed the new fully homomorphism encryption scheme based on the octonion ring over finite field that requires small memory space and complexity to encipher and decipher. It was shown that our scheme is immune from the Gröbner basis attacks by calculating the complexity to obtain the Gröbner basis for the multivariate algebraic equations.

The proposed scheme does not require a "booystrapping" process so that the complexity to encipher and decipher is not large.

§9. Considering composition of plaintext

At end of this chapter we consider the composition of the plaintext.
In section 3 and 4 we adopt $M=(m_0,\dots,m_7) \in O$ as the plaintext where $m_i \in Fq$ $(i=0,\dots,7)$.
The scheme described in section 3 and 4 has the homomorphic property, that is,

$$M=(m_0,\dots,m_7),\ N=(n_0,\dots,n_7)$$

$$E(M,X) + E(N,X) = E(M+N,X) \bmod q,$$

$$E(M,E(N,X)) = E(MN,X) \bmod q.$$

We notice that

$$M+N \bmod q = (m_0,\ldots,m_7) + (n_0,\ldots,n_7) \bmod q$$

$$= (m_0+n_0 \bmod q,\ldots, m_7+n_7 \bmod q).$$

$MN \bmod q$

$$= (\ m_0n_0-m_1n_1- m_2n_2- m_3n_3-m_4n_4- m_5n_5-m_6n_6-m_7n_7 \bmod q,$$

$$m_0n_1+m_1n_0+m_2n_4+m_3n_7-m_4n_2+m_5n_6-m_6n_5-m_7n_3 \bmod q,$$

$$m_0n_2-m_1n_4+m_2n_0+m_3n_5+m_4n_1-m_5n_3+m_6n_7-m_7n_6 \bmod q,$$

$$m_0n_3-m_1n_7-m_2n_5+m_3n_0+m_4n_6+m_5n_2-m_6n_4+m_7n_1 \bmod q,$$

$$m_0n_4+m_1n_2- m_2n_1- m_3n_6+m_4n_0+m_5n_7+m_6n_3- m_7n_5 \bmod q,$$

$$m_0n_5- m_1n_6+m_2n_3- m_3n_2- m_4n_7+m_5n_0+m_6n_1+m_7n_4 \bmod q,$$

$$m_0n_6+m_1n_5- m_2n_7+m_3n_4- m_4n_3- m_5n_1+m_6n_0+m_7n_2 \bmod q,$$

$$m_0n_7+m_1n_3+m_2n_6- m_3n_1+m_4n_5- m_5n_4- m_6n_2+m_7n_0 \bmod q).$$

From the viewpoint of m_i and n_i, it is not clear that this scheme has multiplicative homomorphism.

For practical use, we can also adopt the following method to have the multiplicative homomorphism clearly.

We select the element $B=(b_0,\ldots,b_7)\in O$ such that,

$$L_B := |B|^2 = b_0^2+b_1^2+\ldots+b_7^2 \bmod q = 0,$$

and

$$b_0 \neq 0 \bmod q.$$

We define the partial set of O, S_B by

$$S_B := \{B=(b_0,\ldots,b_7)\in O \mid |B|^2 = b_0^2+b_1^2+\ldots+b_7^2 \bmod q = 0,\ b_0 \neq 0 \bmod q \}.$$

Let u be the plaintext to belong to the set of the plaintext $P=\{u \mid u \in Fq\}$.

Let $v \in Fq$ be the random number.

We define the medium text M by

$$M := u\mathbf{1}+vB \in O,$$

and

$$|M|^2 = (u+vb_0)^2 + v^2(b_1^2 + \ldots + b_7^2) \neq 0 \bmod q.$$

Then

$$u^2 + 2vb_0u + v^2(b_0^2 + b_1^2 + \ldots + b_7^2) \neq 0 \bmod q,$$

$$(u + 2vb_0)\, u \neq 0 \bmod q,$$

We have

$$u \neq 0 \bmod q$$

and

$$u + 2vb_0 \neq 0 \bmod q.$$

Theorem 4.12

$$M^q = (u1 + vB)^q \bmod q = M = u1 + vB \in O,$$

(*Proof.*)

From Theorem 4.3

$$B^2 = -L1 + 2\,b_0B = 2\,b_0B \bmod q,$$

$$M^2 = (u1 + vB)\,(u1 + vB) \bmod q,$$

$$= u^21 + (uv + vu)B + v^2B^2 \bmod q,$$

$$= u^21 + (2uv + 2\,b_0v^2)B \bmod q \bmod q,$$

$$M^3 = (u^21 + (2uv + 2\,b_0v^2)B)\,(u1 + vB) \bmod q,$$

$$= u^31 + (3u^2v + 2\,b_0uv^2 + 2\,b_0\,(2uv + 2\,b_0v^2)v)B \bmod q,$$

$$= u^31 + (3u^2v + 3(2\,b_0)uv^2 + (2\,b_0)^2v^3)B \bmod q,$$

$$M^4 = (u^31 + (3u^2v + 3(2\,b_0)uv^2 + (2\,b_0)^2v^3)B)\,(u1 + vB) \bmod q,$$

$$= u^41 + (4u^3v + 4(2\,b_0)u^2v^2 + 4(2\,b_0)^2uv^3 + (2\,b_0)^3v^4)B \bmod q,$$

$$\ldots \qquad \ldots \qquad \ldots$$

$$M^q = u^q1 + (qu^{q-1}v + q(2\,b_0)u^{q-2}v^2 + \ldots + q(2\,b_0)^{q-2}uv^{q-1} + (2\,b_0)^{q-1}v^q)B \bmod q$$

$$= u\mathbf{1} + (2\ b_0)^{q-1} v^q B \bmod q.$$

Because $(2\ b_0)^{q-1} = 1 \bmod q$ and $v^q = v \bmod q$,

we have

$$M^q = u\mathbf{1} + vB = M \bmod q. \qquad\qquad \text{q.e.d.}$$

Lemma 4.7

$$M_1 M_2 = u_1 u_2 \mathbf{1} + (u_1 v_2 + v_1 u_2 + 2 v_1 v_2\ b_0) B \bmod q$$

where

$$M_1 = (u_1 \mathbf{1} + v_1 B),$$

$$M_2 = (u_2 \mathbf{1} + v_2 B).$$

(*proof*)

$$M_1 M_2 = (u_1 \mathbf{1} + v_1 B)\ (\mathrm{u} m_2 \mathbf{1} + v_2 B)$$

$$= u_1 u_2 \mathbf{1} + (u_1 v_2 + v_1 u_2) B + v_1 v_2 B^2$$

From $B^2 = 2\ b_0 B \bmod q$,

$$= u_1 u_2 \mathbf{1} + (u_1 v_2 + v_1 u_2) B + v_1 v_2 2\ b_0 \mathrm{B}$$

$$= u_1 u_2 \mathbf{1} + (u_1 v_2 + v_1 u_2 + 2 v_1 v_2\ b_0) B \qquad \text{q.e.d.}$$

Here we consider the multiplicative operation on the ciphertexts.
From section 3 "Multiplication scheme on ciphertexts" we have

$$C_1(C_2(X)) \bmod q = E(M_1 , E\ (M_2, X)) \bmod q$$

where

$$C_1(X) = E(M_1, X) = A_1(\ldots(A_k(M_l(A_k^{-1}\ (\ldots(A_1^{-1} X)\ldots) \bmod q$$

and

$$C_2(X) = E\ (M_2, X) = A_1(\ldots(A_k(M_2(A_k^{-1}\ (\ldots(A_1^{-1} X)\ldots) \bmod q$$

are the ciphertexts.

Then we have

$$C_1(C_2(X)) \bmod q = E(M_1 , E\ (M_2, X)) \bmod q$$

$$= A_1(\ldots(A_k(M_1(A_k^{-1}\ (A_1^{-1}(A_1\ (\ldots(A_k(M_2(A_k^{-1}\ (\ldots(A_1^{-1} X)\ldots) \bmod q$$

$$= A_1(\ldots(A_k(M_1(M_2\ (A_k^{-1}\ (\ldots(A_1^{-1} X)\ldots) \bmod q.$$

Substituting $(u_1\mathbf{1}+v_1B)$, $(u_2\mathbf{1}+v_2B)$ to M_1,M_2 we have

$$= A_1(\ldots(A_k((u_1\mathbf{1}+v_1B)\ ((u_2\mathbf{1}+v_2B)\ (A_k^{-1}\ (\ldots(A_1\ ^{-1}X)\ldots)\ \bmod q.$$

$$= A_1(\ldots(A_k((u_1\mathbf{1})((u_2\mathbf{1}+v_2B)\ (A_k^{-1}\ (\ldots(A_1\ ^{-1}X)\ldots)\ \bmod q.$$

$$+ A_1(\ldots(A_k((v_1B)\ ((u_2\mathbf{1}+v_2B)\ (A_k^{-1}\ (\ldots(A_1\ ^{-1}X)\ldots)\ \bmod q.$$

$$= A_1(\ldots(A_k((u_1\mathbf{1})((u_2\mathbf{1})\ (A_k^{-1}\ (\ldots(A_1\ ^{-1}X)\ldots)\ \bmod q.$$

$$+ A_1(\ldots(A_k((u_1\mathbf{1})((v_2B)\ (A_k^{-1}\ (\ldots(A_1\ ^{-1}X)\ldots)\ \bmod q$$

$$+ A_1(\ldots(A_k((v_1B)\ ((m_2\mathbf{1})\ (A_k^{-1}\ (\ldots(A_1\ ^{-1}X)\ldots)\ \bmod q$$

$$+ A_1(\ldots(A_k((v_1B)\ ((v_2B)\ (A_k^{-1}\ (\ldots(A_1\ ^{-1}X)\ldots)\ \bmod q.$$

$$= A_1(\ldots(A_k((u_1u_2\mathbf{1})\ (A_k^{-1}\ (\ldots(A_1\ ^{-1}X)\ldots)\ \bmod q.$$

$$+ A_1(\ldots(A_k((u_1v_2B)\ (A_k^{-1}\ (\ldots(A_1\ ^{-1}X)\ldots)\ \bmod q.$$

$$+ A_1(\ldots(A_k((v_1u_2B)\ (A_k^{-1}\ (\ldots(A_1\ ^{-1}X)\ldots)\ \bmod q$$

$$+ A_1(\ldots(A_k((v_1v_2B\ B)\ (A_k^{-1}\ (\ldots(A_1\ ^{-1}X)\ldots)\ \bmod q.$$

$$= A_1(\ldots(A_k((u_1u_2\mathbf{1}+ u_1v_2B + v_1u_2B + v_1v_2B\ B)\ (A_k^{-1}\ (\ldots(A_1\ ^{-1}X)\ldots)\ \bmod q$$

$$= A_1(\ldots(A_k([u_1u_2\mathbf{1}+ (u_1v_2 + v_1u_2 +2b_0\ v_1v_2)B]\ (A_k^{-1}\ (\ldots(A_1\ ^{-1}X)\ldots)\ \bmod q.$$

Then we have

$$C_1(C_2(X))\ \bmod q = E(M_1 ,E\ (M_2,X))\ \bmod q$$

$$= E((u_1\mathbf{1}+v_1B) ,E\ ((u_2\mathbf{1}+v_2B),X))\ \bmod q$$

$$= E((u_1u_2\mathbf{1}+ (u_1v_2 + v_1u_2 +2b_0\ v_1v_2)B) , X))\ \bmod q.$$

It is shown that in this method we have the multiplicative homomorphism on the plaintext u clearly.

【Explanation of the figure】

　【Fig.4.1】the conceptual chart of the proposed fully homomorphic encryption
　　　scheme
　　【Explanation on symbol】
　　　　100…cloud data centre
　　　　200…device for communicating of user A to be data holder
　　　　300…device for communicating of user B who is a corporation which
　　　　performs data-processing statistically
　　　　400…insecure communication line

　【Fig.4.2】the conceptual chart of the proposed re-encryption scheme
　　【Explanation on symbol】
　　　　100…cloud data centre
　　　　200…device for communicating of user A to be data holder
　　　　300…device for communicating of user B who wants to obtain the raw
　　　　data(plaintext) of the ciphertexts
　　　　400…insecure communication line

Fig.4.1 the conceptual chart of proposed fully homomorphic data-
processing procedure

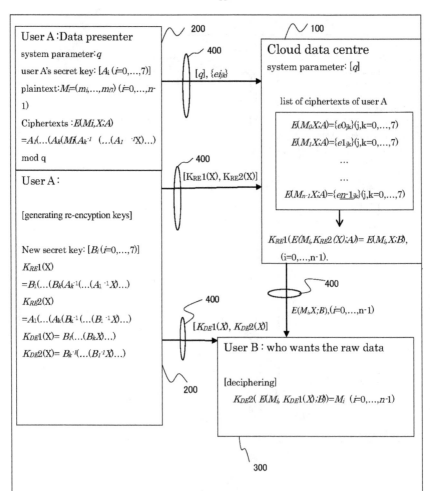

User A : Data presenter

system parameter: q

user A's secret key: $[A_i\ (i=0,\ldots,7)]$

plaintext: $M_i=(m_i,\ldots,m_n)\ (i=0,\ldots,n\text{-}1)$

Ciphertexts : $E(M_i,X;A)$

$=A_i(\ldots(A_k(M_i)A_k^{-1}\ (\ldots(A_1{}^{-1}X)\ldots)$ mod q

User A :

[generating re-encryption keys]

New secret key: $[B_i\ (i=0,\ldots,7)]$

$K_{RE}1(X)$

$=B_1(\ldots(B_k(A_k^{-1}(\ldots(A_1{}^{-1}X)\ldots)$

$K_{RE}2(X)$

$=A_1(\ldots(A_k(B_k^{-1}(\ldots(B_1{}^{-1}X)\ldots)$

$K_{DE}1(X)= B_i(\ldots(B_kX)\ldots)$

$K_{DE}2(X)= B_k^{-1}(\ldots(B_1^{-1}X)\ldots)$

200

400

$[q],\ \{e_{ijk}\}$

400

$[K_{RE}1(X),\ K_{RE}2(X)]$

400

$[K_{DE}1(X),\ K_{DE}2(X)]$

200

Cloud data centre

system parameter: $[q]$

list of ciphertexts of user A

$E(M_0,X;A)=\{e0_{jk}\}(j,k=0,\ldots,7)$

$E(M_1,X;A)=\{e1_{jk}\}(j,k=0,\ldots,7)$

$\ldots$

$\ldots$

$E(M_{n\text{-}1},X;A)=\{e\underline{n\text{-}1}_{jk}\}(j,k=0,\ldots,7)$

$K_{RE}1(E(M_i,K_{RE}2(X);A)=E(M_i,X;B)$, $(i=0,\ldots,n\text{-}1)$.

400

$E(M_i,X;B),(i=0,\ldots,n\text{-}1)$

User B : who wants the raw data

[deciphering]

$K_{DE}2(\ E(M_i,\ K_{DE}1(X);B)=M_i\ (i=0,\ldots,n\text{-}1)$

300

Fig.4.2 the conceptual chart of the proposed re-encryption scheme

BIBLIOGRAPHY

[0.1]   W. Diffie and M. Hellman, "New Directions in Cryptography",
IEEE Transactions on Information Theory, IT-22, 6 , pp.644-654 (Nov.1976)

[0.2] R. L. Rivest , A. Shamir , and L. Adleman, "A Method for Obtaining Digital Signatures and Public-Key Cryptosystems, ", Comm., ACM, Vol.21, No.2, pp.120-126, 1978.2.

[0.3] T. E. ElGamal, "A public key Cryptosystem and a Signature Scheme Based on Discrete Logarithm ", Proceeding Crypto 84 (Aug.1984).

[0.4] N, Koblitz , Translated by Sakurai Kouiti , "A Course in Number Theory and Cryptography ", Springer-Verlag Tokyo, Inc., Tokyo, 1997.

[0.5] Shigeo Tsujii , Kohtaro Tadaki , Masahito Gotaishi ,Ryo Fujita ,and Masao Kasahara ,"Proposal Integrated MPKC:PPS—STS Enhanced Perturbed Piece in Hand Method---," IEICE Tech. Rep.ISEC2009-27,SITE2009-19,ICSS2009-41(2009-07),July 2009.

[0.6] Masahiro Yagisawa, "Proposal for New Key Agreement Protocol ", LAP LAMBERT Academic Publishing GmbH & Co.KG, Germany, June 2011.

[0.7] Masahiro Yagisawa, " Key Agreement Protocol Based on Multivariate Algebraic Equations on Quaternion Ring ",Cryptology ePrint Archive, Report 2010/377,(2010-07). Available at http://eprint.iacr.org/2010/377.

[0.8] Masahiro Yagisawa, "Key Agreement Protocol Using Multivariate Equations on Non-commutative Ring", Cryptology ePrint Archive, Report 2010/458, (2010-08). Available at http://eprint.iacr.org/2010/458.

[0.9] Craig Gentry. Fully Homomorphic Encryption Using Ideal Lattices.In the 41st ACM Symposium on Theory of Computing (STOC), 2009.

[0.10] John H. Conway, Derek A. Smith co-authored, translated by Syuuji Yamada, "On Quaternions and Octonions " Baifuukan Publication Center, Tokyo, .2006.

[1.1] M. Bardet, J. C. Faugere, and B. Salvy, "On the complexity of Gröbner basis computation of semi-regular overdetermined algebraic equations," Proceeding of the International Conference on Polynomial System   Solving(ICPSS2004), pp.71-75, November 2004.

[2.1] R. L. Rivest, L. Adleman, and M. L. Dertouzos.   On data banks and privacy homomorphisms.   In Foundations of Secure Computation, 1978.

[2.2] http://www-03.ibm.com/press/us/en/pressrelease/27840.wss

[2.3] Michael Cooney (2009-06-25). ""IBM touts encryption innovation". Computer World. Retrieved 2009-07-14.

[2.4] Damien Stehle; Ron Steinfeld (2010-05-19). "Faster Fully Homomorphic Encryption" (PDF). International Association for Cryptologic Research. Retrieved 2010-09-15.

[2.5] Craig Gentry, A Fully Homomorphic Encryption Scheme, 2009. Available at http://crypto.stanford.edu/craig/craig-thesis.pdf .

[2.6] Craig Gentry. "Computing Arbitrary Functions of Encrypted Data". Association for Computing Machinery.

[2.7] Marten van Dijk; Craig Gentry, Shai Halevi, and Vinod Vaikuntanathan (2009-12-11). "Fully Homomorphic Encryption over the Integers" (PDF). International Association for Cryptologic Research. Retrieved 2010-03-18.

[2.8] Bram Cohen. "Simple Public Key Encryption". Available at http://en.wikipedia.org/wiki/Cohen's_cryptosystem .

[2.9] JS Coron, A Mandal, D Naccache, M Tibouchi ," Fully homomorphic encryption over the integers with shorter public keys", Advances in Cryptology–CRYPTO 2011, 487-504.

[2.10] Halevi, Shai. "An Implementation of homomorphic encryption". Retrieved 30 April 2013. Available at https://github.com/shaih/HElib .

[2.11] Nuida and Kurosawa,"(Batch) Fully Homomorphic Encryption over Integers for Non-Binary Message Spaces", Cryptology ePrint Archive, Report 2014/777, 2014. http://eprint.iacr.org/.

[4.1] T. Matsumoto, H. Imai, H. Harashima, and H. Miyakawa, "A class of asymmetric cryptosystems using obscure representations of enciphering functions, " in 1983 National Convention Record on Information Systems, IECE Japan, 1983.

[4.2] T. Matsumoto, and H. Imai, "Public quadratic polynomial-tuples for efficient signature verification and message-encryption," Lecture Notes in Computer Science on Advances in Cryptology-EUROCRYPT'88, pp.419–453, New York, NY, USA, 1988, Springer-Verlag New York, Inc.

[4.3] S. Tsujii, K. Tadaki, and R. Fujita, "Piece in hand concept for enhancing the security of multivariate type public key cryptosystems: Public key without containing all the information of secret key," Cryptology ePrint Archive, Report 2004/366, 2004.

[4.4] C.Wolf, and B. Preneel, "Taxonomy of public key schemes based on the problem of multivariate quadratic equations," Cryptology ePrint Archive, Report 2005/077, 2005, http://eprint.iacr.org/.

[4.5] Shigeo Tsujii , Kohtaro Tadaki , Masahito Gotaishi ,Ryo Fujita ,and Masao Kasahara ,"Proposal Integrated MPKC:PPS—STS Enhanced Perturbed Piece in Hand Method---," IEICE Tech. Rep.ISEC2009-27, SITE2009-19, ICSS2009-41(2009-07), July 2009.

Appendix A:

Octinv(*A*) --

$S \leftarrow a_0^2 + a_1^2 + \dots + a_7^2 \bmod q.$

$\% \ S^{-1} \bmod q$

    q[1] ← q div S ;% integer part of q/S

    r[1] ← q mod S ;% residue

    k ←1

    q[0] ← q

    r[0] ← S

    while r[k] ≠ 0

        begin

            k← k + 1

            q[k] ← r[k−2] div r[k−1]

            r[k] ← r[k−2] mod [rk−1]

        end

Q [k−1] ← (-1)*q[k−1]

L[k−1] ← 1

i ← k−1

while   i > 1

    begin

        Q[i−1] ← (-1)*Q[i] *q[i−1] + L[i]

        L[i−1] ← Q[i]

        i← i−1

    end

invS ← Q[1] mod *q*

invA[0] ← a₀*invS mod *q*

For *i*=1,…,7,

    invA[*i*] ← (-1)*aᵢ*invS mod *q*

Return A^{-1} = (invA[0], invA[1],…, invA[7])

Appendix B:

Theorem 4.1

Let $A=(a_{10},a_{11},...,a_{17})\in O$, $a_{1j}\in Fq$ $(j=0,1,...,7)$.

Let $A^n=(a_{n0},a_{n1},...,a_{n7})\in O$, $a_{nj}\in Fq$ $(n=1,...,7;j=0,1,...,7)$.

a_{00} ,a_{nj} 's$(n=1,2,...;j=0,1,...)$and b_n's $(n=0,1,...)$ satisfy the equations such that

$N= a_{11}^2+...+a_{17}^2 \bmod q$

$a_{00}=1$, $b_0=0$, $b_1=1$,

$$a_{n0}= a_{n-1,0}\,a_{10}-b_{n-1}N \bmod q \,,(n=1,2,...) \tag{4.8}$$

$$b_n= a_{n-1,0}+ b_{n-1}a_{10} \bmod q \,,(n=1,2,...) \tag{4.9}$$

$$a_{nj}= b_n a_{1j} \bmod q \,,(n=1,2,...;j=1,2,...,7) . \tag{4.10}$$

(*Proof:*)

We use mathematical induction method.

[step 1]

When $n=1$, (4.8) holds because

$a_{10}= a_{00}\,a_{10} - b_0N=a_{10} \bmod q$.

(4.9) holds because

$b_1= a_{00}+ b_0a_{10} =a_{00} =1\bmod q$.

(4.10) holds because

$a_{1j}= b_1 a_{1j} = a_{1j} \bmod q \,,(j=1,2,...,7)$

[step 2]

When $n=k$,

If it holds that

$a_{k0}= a_{k-1,0}\,a_{10} - b_{k-1}N \bmod q \,,(k=2,3,4,...)$,

$b_k= a_{k-1,0}+ b_{k-1}a_{10} \bmod q$,

$a_{kj}= b_k a_{1j} \bmod q \,,(j=1,2,...,7)$,

from (4.9)

$b_{k-1}= a_{k-2,0}+ b_{k-2}a_{10} \bmod q \,,(k=2,3,4,...)$,

then

$A^{k+1}=A^kA=(a_{k0}, b_ka_{11},..., b_ka_{17})(a_{10},a_{11},...,a_{17})$

$=(a_{k0}\,a_{10} - b_kN, a_{k0}\,a_{11}+ b_ka_{11}\,a_{10},..., a_{k0}\,a_{17}+ b_ka_{17}\,a_{10})$

$=(a_{k0}\,a_{10} - b_kN, (a_{k0} + b_ka_{10})a_{11},..., (a_{k0} + b_ka_{10})a_{17})$

$=(a_{k+1,0}, b_{k+1,0}\,a_{11},..., b_{k+1,0}\,a_{17})$,

as was required.   q.e.d.

Appendix C:

Theorem 4.2

For an element $A=(a_{10}, a_{11}, ..., a_{17}) \in O$,

$A^{J+1} = A \bmod q$,

where

$J := LCM\{q^2-1, q-1\} = q^2-1$,

$N := a_{11}^2 + a_{12}^2 + ... + a_{17}^2 \neq 0 \bmod q$.

(*Proof:*)

From (4.8) and (4.9) it comes that

$a_{n0} = a_{n-1,0} a_{10} - b_{n-1} N \bmod q$,

$b_n = a_{n-1,0} + b_{n-1} a_{10} \bmod q$,

$a_{n0} a_{10} + b_n N = (a_{n-1,0} a_{10} - b_{n-1} N) a_{10} + (a_{n-1,0} + b_{n-1} a_{10}) N = a_{n-1,0} a_{10}^2 + a_{n-1,0} N \bmod q$,

$b_n N = a_{n-1,0} a_{10}^2 + a_{n-1,0} N - a_{n0} a_{10} \bmod q$,

$b_{n-1} N = a_{n-2,0} a_{10}^2 + a_{n-2,0} N - a_{n-1,0} a_{10} \bmod q$,

$a_{n0} = 2 a_{10} a_{n-1,0} - (a_{10}^2 + N) a_{n-2,0} \bmod q$, $(n=1,2,...)$.

1) In case that $-N \neq 0 \bmod q$ is quadratic non-residue of prime q,

Because $-N \neq 0 \bmod q$ is quadratic non-residue of prime q,

$(-N)^{(q-1)/2} = -1 \bmod q$.

$a_{n0} - 2 a_{10} a_{n-1,0} + (a_{10}^2 + N) a_{n-2,0} = 0 \bmod q$,

$a_{n0} = (\beta^n (a_{10}-\alpha) + (\beta - a_{10}) \alpha^n)/(\beta - \alpha)$ over $Fq[\alpha]$

$b_n = (\beta^n - \alpha^n)/(\beta - \alpha)$ over $Fq[\alpha]$

where α, β are roots of algebraic quadratic equation such that

$t^2 - 2a_{10}t + a_{10}^2 + N = 0$.

$\alpha = a_{10} + \sqrt{-N}$ over $Fq[\alpha]$,

$\beta = a_{10} - \sqrt{-N}$ over $Fq[\alpha]$.

We can calculate β^{q^2} as follows.

$\beta^{q^2} = (a_{10} - \sqrt{-N})^{q^2}$ over $Fq[\alpha]$

$= (a_{10}^q - \sqrt{-N}(-N)^{(q-1)/2})^q$ over $Fq[\alpha]$

$$= (a_{10} - \sqrt{-N}(-N)^{(q-1)/2})^q \; over \; Fq[\alpha]$$

$$= (a_{10}{}^q - \sqrt{-N}(-N)^{(q-1)/2}(-N)^{(q-1)/2}) \; over \; Fq[\alpha]$$

$$= a_{10} - \sqrt{-N}(-1)(-1) \quad over \; \textbf{Fq}[\alpha]$$
$$= a_{10} - \sqrt{-N} \; over \; \textbf{Fq}[\alpha]$$
$$= \beta \; over \; Fq[\alpha].$$

In the same manner we obtain

$$\alpha^{q^2} = \alpha \; over \; \textbf{Fq}[\alpha].$$

$$a_{q^2,0} = (\beta^{q^2}(a_{10} - \alpha) + (\beta - a_{10})\alpha^{q^2})/(\beta - \alpha)$$

$$= (\beta(a_{10}-\alpha) + (\beta- a_{10})\alpha)/(\beta- \alpha) = a_{10} \mod q.$$

$$b_{q^2} = (\beta^{q^2} - \alpha^{q^2})/(\beta - \alpha) = 1 \mod q.$$

Then we obtain

$$A^{q2} = (a_{q2,0}, b_{q2}a_{11}, ..., b_{q2}a_{17})$$
$$= (a_{10}, a_{11}, ..., a_{17}) = A \mod q$$

2) In case that $-N \neq 0 \mod q$ is quadratic residue of prime q

$a_{n0} = (\beta^n(a_{10}-\alpha) + (\beta- a_{10})\alpha^n)/(\beta- \alpha) \quad \mod q,$

$b_{n0} = (\beta^n - \alpha^n)/(\beta- \alpha) \quad \mod q,$

As $\alpha, \beta \in \textbf{Fq}$, from Fermat's little Theorem

$\beta^q = \beta \mod q,$

$\alpha^q = \alpha \mod q.$

Then we have

$a_{q0} = (\beta^q(a_{10}-\alpha) + (\beta- a_{10})\alpha^q)/(\beta- \alpha) \mod q$

$= (\beta(a_{10}-\alpha) + (\beta- a_{10})\alpha)/(\beta- \alpha) \mod q$

$= a_{10} \mod q$

$b_q = (\beta^q - \alpha^q)/(\beta- \alpha) = 1 \mod q.$

Then we have

$a^q = (a_{q0}, b_q a_{11}, ..., b_q a_{17})$

$= (a_{10}, a_{11}, ..., a_{17}) = a \mod q.$

We therefore arrive at the equation such as

$A^{J+1}=A \bmod q$ for arbitrary element $A \in O$,

where

$$J= \text{LCM} \{ q^2-1,q-1\}=q^2-1,$$

as was required.   q.e.d.

We notice that

in case that $-N=0 \bmod q$

$a_{00}=1,\ b_0=0,\ b_1=1,$

From (4.8)

$a_{n0}= a_{n-1,0}\,a_{10} \bmod q\ ,(n=1,2,\ldots),$

then we have

$a_{n0}= a_{10}{}^n \bmod q\ ,(n=1,2,\ldots).$

$a_{q0}= a_{10}{}^q= a_{10} \bmod q.$

From (4.9),

$b_n= a_{n-1,0}+ b_{n-1}a_{10} \bmod q\ ,(n=1,2,\ldots)$

$= a_{10}{}^{n-1}+ b_{n-1}a_{10} \bmod q$

$= 2a_{10}{}^{n-1}+ b_{n-2}a_{10}{}^2 \bmod q$

$\cdots \qquad \cdots$

$= (n-1)a_{10}{}^{n-1}+ b_1 a_{10}{}^{n-1} \bmod q$

$= na_{10}{}^{n-1} \bmod q.$

Then we have

$a_{nj}= na_{10}{}^{n-1}a_{1j} \bmod q\ ,(n=1,2,\ldots;j=1,2,\ldots,7)\ .$

$a_{qj}= qa_{10}{}^{q-1}a_{1j} \bmod q =0,(\,j=1,2,\ldots,7)\ .$

Appendix D:

Lemma 4.2

$$A^{-1}(AB) = B$$
$$(BA)A^{-1} = B$$

(Proof:)

$A^{-1} = (a_0/|A|^2 \bmod q, -a_1/|A|^2 \bmod q, \ldots, -a_7/|A|^2 \bmod q).$

$AB \bmod q$

$= (\ a_0b_0 - a_1b_1 - a_2b_2 - a_3b_3 - a_4b_4 - a_5b_5 - a_6b_6 - a_7b_7 \bmod q,$

$\quad a_0b_1 + a_1b_0 + a_2b_4 + a_3b_7 - a_4b_2 + a_5b_6 - a_6b_5 - a_7b_3 \bmod q,$

$\quad a_0b_2 - a_1b_4 + a_2b_0 + a_3b_5 + a_4b_1 - a_5b_3 + a_6b_7 - a_7b_6 \bmod q,$

$\quad a_0b_3 - a_1b_7 - a_2b_5 + a_3b_0 + a_4b_6 + a_5b_2 - a_6b_4 + a_7b_1 \bmod q,$

$\quad a_0b_4 + a_1b_2 - a_2b_1 - a_3b_6 + a_4b_0 + a_5b_7 + a_6b_3 - a_7b_5 \bmod q,$

$\quad a_0b_5 - a_1b_6 + a_2b_3 - a_3b_2 - a_4b_7 + a_5b_0 + a_6b_1 + a_7b_4 \bmod q,$

$\quad a_0b_6 + a_1b_5 - a_2b_7 + a_3b_4 - a_4b_3 - a_5b_1 + a_6b_0 + a_7b_2 \bmod q,$

$\quad a_0b_7 + a_1b_3 + a_2b_6 - a_3b_1 + a_4b_5 - a_5b_4 - a_6b_2 + a_7b_0 \bmod q).$

$[A^{-1}(AB)]_0$

$= \{\ a_0(a_0b_0 - a_1b_1 - a_2b_2 - a_3b_3 - a_4b_4 - a_5b_5 - a_6b_6 - a_7b_7)$

$\quad + a_1(a_0b_1 + a_1b_0 + a_2b_4 + a_3b_7 - a_4b_2 + a_5b_6 - a_6b_5 - a_7b_3)$

$\quad + a_2(a_0b_2 - a_1b_4 + a_2b_0 + a_3b_5 + a_4b_1 - a_5b_3 + a_6b_7 - a_7b_6)$

$\quad + a_3(a_0b_3 - a_1b_7 - a_2b_5 + a_3b_0 + a_4b_6 + a_5b_2 - a_6b_4 + a_7b_1)$

$\quad + a_4(a_0b_4 + a_1b_2 - a_2b_1 - a_3b_6 + a_4b_0 + a_5b_7 + a_6b_3 - a_7b_5)$

$\quad + a_5(a_0b_5 - a_1b_6 + a_2b_3 - a_3b_2 - a_4b_7 + a_5b_0 + a_6b_1 + a_7b_4)$

$\quad + a_6(a_0b_6 + a_1b_5 - a_2b_7 + a_3b_4 - a_4b_3 - a_5b_1 + a_6b_0 + a_7b_2)$

$\quad + a_7(a_0b_7 + a_1b_3 + a_2b_6 - a_3b_1 + a_4b_5 - a_5b_4 - a_6b_2 + a_7b_0)\} / |A|^2 \bmod q$

$= \{(\ a_0^2 + a_1^2 + \ldots + a_7^2)\ b_0\} / |A|^2 = b_0 \bmod q$

where $[M]_n$ denotes the n-th element of $M \in O.$

$[A^{-1}(AB)]_1$

$= \{\ a_0(a_0b_1 + a_1b_0 + a_2b_4 + a_3b_7 - a_4b_2 + a_5b_6 - a_6b_5 - a_7b_3)$

$\quad - a_1(a_0b_0 - a_1b_1 - a_2b_2 - a_3b_3 - a_4b_4 - a_5b_5 - a_6b_6 - a_7b_7)$

$\quad - a_2(a_0b_4 + a_1b_2 - a_2b_1 - a_3b_6 + a_4b_0 + a_5b_7 + a_6b_3 - a_7b_5)$

$-a_3(a_0b_7+a_1b_3+a_2b_6-a_3b_1+a_4b_5-a_5b_4-a_6b_2+a_7b_0)$

$+a_4(a_0b_2-a_1b_4+a_2b_0+a_3b_5+a_4b_1-a_5b_3+a_6b_7-a_7b_6)$

$- a_5(a_0b_6+a_1b_5-a_2b_7+a_3b_4-a_4b_3-a_5b_1+a_6b_0+a_7b_2)$

$+a_6(a_0b_5-a_1b_6+a_2b_3-a_3b_2-a_4b_7+a_5b_0+a_6b_1+a_7b_4\ )$

$+a_7(a_0b_3-a_1b_7-a_2b_5+a_3b_0+a_4b_6+a_5b_2-a_6b_4+a_7b_1)\} \ /|A|^2 \bmod q$

$=\{(\ a_0^2+a_1^2+\ldots+a_7^2)\ b_1\} \ /|A|^2=b_1 \bmod q.$

Similarly we have

$[A^{-1}(AB)]_i=b_i \bmod q \ (i=2,3,\ldots,7).$

Then

$$A^{-1}(AB)= B \bmod q. \qquad \text{q.e.d.}$$